The Whole Woman

Ezekiel Azonwu and Kiyanna Azonwu

Published by One Vision Publishing LLC, 2019.

While every precaution has been taken in the preparation of this book, the publisher assumes no responsibility for errors or omissions, or for damages resulting from the use of the information contained herein.

THE WHOLE WOMAN

First edition. August 29, 2019

Contribution and Arrangement by Brandon Epps

Contribution by Milan Epps

Book Cover Design by Justin Foster

Graphic Design by Jarvis Williams

Photography by Alex Rogers

ISBN: 978-1733419901 (Paperback)

ISBN: 978-1733419918 (ebook)

Published by One Vision Publishing LLC, 2019.

www.thewholelifenow.com

This book is dedicated to our 5 beautiful children.

Without them, we would lack the fuel to show the world what God's love looks like.

Chapter 1: We Are All Broken

———

"And he said unto him, Arise, go your way: your faith has made you whole."

Luke 17:19

In today's society, it's more than fair to say that most of us experience our share of emotional issues and hardships when it comes to connecting with others. Even when we make a concerted effort to be outgoing or great active listeners. Even when we smile or pretend to laugh at jokes we don't understand (or that simply aren't funny). Even when we clear our schedules to make time for others or go out of our way to be helpful or sympathetic. Even with all of that, it can become exhausting trying to make strong connections with other people. And if making friends is difficult, finding a romantic partner to spend the rest of our lives with can seem downright impossible.

But why does it have to be so hard to find that other half who will comfort us in those trying times and support us as we navigate through the convoluted experience we call life? Why is it such a task discovering that person that God has created to complete the half-finished jigsaw puzzle that we are?

Let's consider the possibility that the question itself is also the answer. Maybe the concept of our other half (which many refer to as their better half) is the reason we can't find a whole relationship. Perhaps instead of looking for half of a relationship to fit perfectly with our half, we need to consider the idea that our first objective should be to become a whole person; because if we are whole, then we have no need for half of a relationship to complete us. If we are whole, only a whole relationship will do, and as a whole child of God, we'll find less of a struggle attracting that whole man that God is willing to send our way.

Now, we can only imagine what you're thinking at this point. But for the sake of argument, let's assume it's something along the lines of, "If God has a whole man waiting for me, why not use the man to help me become whole?"

While that is definitely a valid question, we would equate it to asking why not have a straight A student start hanging out with delinquents and high school dropouts in hopes of rubbing off on them one day. It sounds like a novel idea. But there's a good reason why most parents or mentors advise their ambitious or studious children against running in the same circles as the other kids that don't value hard work or lifelong pursuits at learning. And that reason is simple: *It's much easier to drag someone down than it is to build them up.* A student hanging around thugs and neighborhood goons is a lot more likely to pick up their bad habits and views toward life than she is to influence them to turn their lives around and find ways to contribute to their lives and the lives of others in a positive and meaningful way.

So, why would it seem reasonable to send a whole man into the life of a woman who is nowhere near that level of wholeness in her life, and may not even recognize just how much work she needs to do in order to reach a point where she wouldn't risk undoing his self-progression or what was meant to be an amazing relationship?

Let's imagine for a moment that, as a child, you were the kind of person who would thrive on positive feedback. The kind of person who worked their hardest in school and at home; bringing home A's and B's and doing chores often without having to be asked by either of your parents.

But in return for all your hard work, you were lucky to receive any real praise. Not the generic 'good job' that any kid would get just for completing the task (and completing it incorrectly like many do when they don't feel motivated to actually try).

Real praise as in 'Wow! I'm so proud of you! If everyone put in the same effort as you we may just achieve a perfect world! Keep setting an example. Hopefully, everyone else will start to pick up on it and take it to heart like I do.' Follow that with a hug or a loving hand on the shoulder, and ask yourself if that wouldn't make your day.

What we're all looking for is what we like to call *proof of love*. What is proof of love? It's exactly like it sounds. It is proof through action that someone loves you. The saying that actions speak louder than words is not just some tired cliché. It is a powerful proverb that influences both how we see ourselves and how we view and interact with others. Someone can tell you they admire or respect you, but when their actions seem to suggest otherwise, it becomes difficult to believe them.

When you see someone go out of their way to do something for you—without ever asking for anything in return—it becomes much harder to question whether or not they care about you, doesn't it? To quote one more idiom, that's because 'the proof is in the pudding!'

But let's revisit our previous *proof of love* example. Let's imagine that instead of getting that kind of praise you needed to prove that you were appreciated for being such a hard worker, you regularly received the opposite. If every authoritative figure in your life only gave you the same generic 'way to go' or 'keep it up' after all your years of hard work, what might your next move be? It wouldn't be hard to make a shift in your thinking and actions. But one thing is for sure. Your chances of choosing a positive, unwavering path from that point would have become drastically slimmer.

There are too many variations of how someone could come to a point where they feel like they haven't been appreciated (or appreciated enough) to count. And no matter what form of appreciation you feel you've been missing, we all have a proof threshold. When that threshold fails to be reached for too long, the message to our subconscious becomes clear. *We are lacking in something we need and we need to find a way to get it!* Unfortunately, this message is easily paired with a second message:

I don't have what it takes to replace what is missing, so I need to look to other people or things to fill that gap.

This way of thinking sets us down a scary path, because we are then confirming the false assertion that God didn't supply us with the tools to make ourselves happy, which also suggests that we have to look outside of ourselves for the tools to create and maintain the happiness and contentment that we've desperately longed for—all because we're missing that proof of love.

It's pretty easy for this to lead to clingy, desperate, or even aggressive behavior in the dating world. But some of us don't like this disempowering feeling of inadequacy, and will fight to convince ourselves and others that this is not true. In other words, we might become defensive.

Again, there are a myriad of ways in which we might respond to the idea that we aren't enough because we have a problem that we cannot fix on our own. But the first step toward resolution is determining where this problem resides within you. If we can do that then there's more than a little hope for us.

There's opportunity to actualize that higher version of ourselves that God created us to be. There's a brilliant light at the end of the tunnel. There's a lasting sense of peace—even in the midst of adversity. And as a huge bonus, there's harmony between us and our loved ones. And that same harmony is what can either attract the man that God has for you or improve your relationship with the man that is currently in your life.

Why You AREN'T Ready

IT MAY FEEL A BIT MORE encouraging to think that you're far along enough with your own self-development to be the exception. But the chances of that being the case are so extremely low that this statement seems worth making once again. Until you've made significant personal progress toward becoming a more whole person, you aren't ready for the relationship you've been seeking.

Now that we're on the same page, let us also say a few important things that are just as important as the statement you've just read.

1. Just because you may not be ready for that relationship you've been praying for doesn't mean that you aren't worth being loved. In fact, that couldn't be further from the truth. And a very important part of your self-healing and becoming whole is understanding just how worthy of love you already are. But this love first needs to come from within. You must recognize who loved you first with Agape (unconditional love), this is fuel and reason enough for you to love yourself with that same type of love. And once you understand how to love yourself, you will better understand how to feel and show that love for someone else.

2. You may be further along in your process than you realize. But even if you aren't far along enough for that relationship, we all progress at different rates and require varying amounts of focus and attention of key areas of personal weakness. So, just because someone else may have taken some number of months or years to reach a solid personal foundation for a romantic relationship doesn't mean that you will require just

as long as they did.

3. Although a goal is to achieve wholeness and a sense of lasting joy and appreciation within yourself. This doesn't mean that there will be some pinnacle point that you will reach; where you will suddenly be perfect and everything will immediately come to you at that point of completion. Life is a continuous journey. And just because someone else you know may be in the kind of relationship you keep telling yourself that you want, it doesn't mean that they've achieved some elevated level or a wholeness that has thus far evaded your reach. Sure, it is possible that they have been working on themselves and making those difficult and honest decisions based on where they are and what they feel is either missing for them or in need of serious healing. But, like the vast majority of us, they probably still have a fair amount of work to do. And that leads us into the last point.

4. Your goal may be to become a more whole person, but it is essentially an unending journey. To assume that there is a stopping point or specific destination for personal growth is akin to assuming that you can reach a point where you have nothing else in life to learn. If that were the case, I would imagine God wouldn't send for so many opportunities for lessons. If anything, He might even send for us as soon as we reached that point, because there would be nothing else for Him to teach us in this plane of existence. That being said, the fact that you are working to progress is one of the most important parts of becoming ready for that relationship you want. And through that relationship, you will find more opportunities for personal and collective growth. So, if you haven't come to a point of total inner healing, with enough work, you will see and understand that there is a wholeness within you that is as clear as day to yourself and others. And

that will be a huge part of what attracts and fosters a successful relationship between you and that special someone when the time comes. And, if by chance, you're already in a relationship, we would implore you to let this serve as a guide to help you see where you can improve yourself and your relationship until it becomes the kind of relationship that you were made for; the very same relationship that you might not have even realized that your soul was yearning for all along.

What Makes Us Broken?

SO, WHAT MAKES US BROKEN? Are we just born with bad luck? Did our parents ruin us from early childhood and leave us to pick up the pieces? Is our environment the cause? Well, no and yes. And then, yes again. But it's not all on our parents and our environment. Anyone can claim that they are simply a product of their environment and lackluster parenting. But that essentially absolves us of all blame; which isn't fair to our parents, our environment, or ourselves. What's more, it's not entirely accurate anyway. Think about those many stories you've heard over the years, detailing how one person or group accomplished something amazing despite their background or upbringing. In those instances, it came down to a choice. A choice to be better than expected. A choice to do whatever was necessary to accomplish a specific goal or reach new heights. And, one way or another, that choice made all the difference.

In the Garden of Eden, that old serpent slithered in and convinced Eve that God wasn't completely transparent about their true potential as humans.

"For God knows that when you eat of it your eyes will be opened, and you will be like God, knowing good and evil"

Genesis 3:5

Satan appealed to a desire that God formed in every man and woman from the beginning. Our desire to be satisfied to the highest degree. He suggested that once they disobeyed they could replace the very God who kept them from breaking. And until this day we are fallen, attempting to replace the God who makes us whole. Because we were all born into sin, brokenness has essentially become a rite of passage for humanity. Despite how it happens, it will happen, and there's nothing we can do about that.

When I (Kiyanna) met Ezekiel, he was so in love with everything I did and said. He would often break the mood of our moments and ask, "What's wrong with you?" It never ceased to shock me. But he would further explain that he was certain that I had to have some type of flaw or issue that would make me less perfect and more human in his eyes. I would always respond with, "just wait, you'll see". We may have shattered differently but our pieces will be restored together. There are many factors that collectively contribute to anyone or anything becoming who or what they become. Haven't you ever heard the phrase 'it takes a village?' Those words ring truer than you may realize. And your life was no exception. Despite any number of factors that you have in common with someone else you may know, you didn't turn out exactly the same, did you? Yeah, didn't think so.

Although we'll go into greater detail about this in the coming chapters, we feel it will only serve to benefit you to provide a bit more background on how else we become broken, and the signs that you might be exampling without even realizing it. So, let's go over a few of the heavier influences that contribute to someone becoming broken.

Contributing Factors

IT IS HUMAN NATURE to want to bond with other people. Building relationships is essential to our growth and development as individuals and as a community. But for all the good it can bring, there is also room for a downside to this. For many of us that comes in the form of seeking acceptance and acknowledgement from others.

It starts with our parents. As toddlers, we perform little tricks like scribbling on paper, performing some simple not-quite-acrobatic jump or roll, or playing with our toys. We often try to either show our parents what we've done or get them to join in on the fun. Either way, what we're really looking for is our parents' approval; some sign that what we're doing is not only okay, but it's worth their undivided attention and adoration.

This, of course, progresses as we venture out into school and interact with other children and teachers. We often find ourselves working hard to identify potential friends and then put in the effort to turn these strangers and acquaintances into friends. In earlier grades, our efforts tend to be much easier as most small children don't have to think all that extensively about what we bring to the table in a friendship. They are more willing to make that leap of faith that we know how to be a good friend and are therefore open to seeing what comes of this new bond.

It's only in later years that judgment and deliberation take such a heavy role in the process of applying for new friends and accepting the verbal applications of others. In these scenarios, the mutual benefit needs to be clearer to us or else we're much more hesitant to either reject the friendship or to keep someone at a distance; allowing them to be called our friend, but with conditions and a multitude of restrictions we would never impose on a best friend or someone we were even remotely romantically interested in.

But as time goes on, we start finding more and more of our conditions getting in the way of fostering the kinds of relationships we say we want. And we can't even begin to understand why or how to build these relationships in a fulfilling or even satisfactory way. We may want to blame everyone else for being weird or stubborn or misaligned with what we want from the relationship (all of which could be a factor), but we should also take each failed relationship or awkward falling out as a chance to look within and ask if there was anything about ourselves that might've allowed that exchange to go any smoother. And our failure to ask these kinds of questions (or to even recognize that these questions could've been asked) is often another sign that we are experiencing a symptom of being broken.

But let us be clear in saying that the need for having others to interact with is Godly. This desire for connection is not something that shackles us, but something that helps to unify us; we were built for community. Human bonds, therefore, are an undeniable part of who we are both individually and collectively.

Of course, this desire has propelled us to create harmony through fellowship (whether in or out of a church setting) and to foster loving relationships with more of our sisters and brothers in Christ. But there also came a downside for us at any time that one of these relationships fell through. Often that downside was exampled in our attempts to fill whatever void was left in place of the friendship or relationship. This is likely due to the saying that nature abhors vacuums (no, not the electronic appliances. Though, we'd imagine the noise would be offputting). This is exemplified in Genesis 2:18:

> *"The LORD God said, "It is not good for the man to be alone. I will make a companion for him who corresponds to him."*

Even here, it is clear that God did not intend for us to be alone throughout our lives. We were meant to connect with others and unify with more of His wonderful creations. But the other downside of this is that we tend to consciously or subconsciously take many of the failed relationships as an indicator or supporter of the idea that something is wrong with us. But that couldn't be further from the truth. Even if we have more work to do to improve our approach and response to others, that doesn't indicate that we are unworthy of communing with others. What it does indicate to us, however, is that we are showing symptoms of brokenness.

There are, of course, multiple ways to become broken. And we believe that each of them stems from a lack of emotional support in one or more ways. A strong emotional foundation is a critical part of our development from early childhood well into adulthood. Lacking this emotional foundation will inevitably lead to becoming broken because there is no other means of affirming our value ourselves. Another way of seeing this need to affirm our value is through the expectations we hold as we go through life. Based on the feedback we receive from our environment and other people; those expectations can change for better or for worse. And with each change, we either come one step closer to wholeness or deepen the cracks of brokenness within us.

But that's the beauty of it all. Sure, we could see examples such as these as confirmation that we must begrudgingly accept responsibility for how our lives turned out. But this also means that you already have what you need to create that amazing and purpose filled life that God has prepared for you. And the heart of this book is to help bridge the gap between where you are and where you are meant to be after taking stock of what needs to be healed and then putting in the work to actually address it.

We generally like to have some idea of where we're going (or at least where we'd like to be) before we start moving in any direction. So, before we move on, let's take a brief moment to imagine what we would like to achieve here. "Why imagine," you may be asking? Because if we can create that picture in our minds and hold it for a few seconds, our conscious (and subconscious) will have something to grasp at and reference when the road toward our sense of harmony and wholeness become challenged from internal and external factors. Having a clear idea of how you would like to see yourself allows you to ask the necessary questions and take the small, yet vital steps to get there without compromising the effort or end result. That is true success. That is true accomplishment. And if you stick with us for the duration of this book, soon you'll be looking at yourself in the mirror and honestly saying, "That is me."

With that said, we'd like to invite you to spend the next sixty seconds (after reading this paragraph, of course) quietly answering these simple, powerful questions to yourself:

- What does a true smile look like for me (imagine yourself in some place that you usually enjoy being with a warm smile on your face. This should come from deep within your heart and be a joyful smile)?
- Why am I smiling (what is causing a feeling within you that is overflowing so much that you can't help but smile. This is not a judgment exercise. So, it can be anything)?
- How can you create this feeling for yourself and help to nurture it in others (the answer to this should be simple)? For example, smiling at people more often, offering a helping hand when you see someone in need, or saying something nice to yourself and others more often)?
- What would it feel like to have this same sense of peace and joy when I'm by myself?

- What would it feel like to have this same sense of peace and joy when I'm with someone I really care about (again, no need to think too hard here. The feeling is most important)?

Once you've got that feeling flowing through you, try and let that feeling run through your mind and heart for the next sixty seconds. And at the end of that sixty seconds, remind yourself that you deserve to feel this way as much as possible, and thank God our heavenly father for allowing you to experience this profound blessing.

One thing to bear in mind is that you don't need to attach an image of anyone in particular when imagining. If it makes the process even the slightest bit more difficult (or if you find yourself thinking about someone that either doesn't feel the same way or gives you doubts about whether or not the two of you are meant to be), let the visage of a specific person go. You'll probably find that the process is significantly easier and more effective for you. Again, we're placing our greatest focus on the image of yourself and the happy feeling that accompanies that.

But while we're here, we would like to encourage your focus on your passion and purpose through the spirit of God.

Evidence of Your Brokenness

OUR DESIRE FOR LOVE can drive us to act out with others in various ways. We generally tend to associate the phrase 'acting out' as a negative term; often used to describe the actions of a child's tantrum. But although acting out tends to be thought of as a prelude to acting out of the norm or acting outside of an allowed behavior, for the sake of approaching our argument from an objective standpoint, we would invite you to think of acting out as more of a prelude to the phrase acting out of a desire for something that you fear you won't receive.

If that is the case, then even the behavior of a child begins to make more sense. In this way of thinking, it would seem a bit rare to find someone who acts undesirably with others without some sense of motivated due cause. We would argue that more than 95% of all acting out scenarios are born of a motivation, whether clear or unclear. We simply need to take a moment to assess the situation and ask the necessary questions first.

But allow us to also be clear in saying that just because there is due cause to someone's actions doesn't automatically make the actions permissible. It does however, allow light to be shed on this situation in a more patient, objective, and empathetic manner; which can go a long way to resolving it in both the short and long term.

The desire to receive the proof of love that best fills you can lead to various approaches to love that may be interpreted as a cry for wholeness. But make no mistake, being with someone who isn't exhibiting that proof of love in the way that you desire can be the catalyst to any of these behaviors. In the same vein, not fulfilling someone else's proof of love in the way that is the clearest and most fulfilling to them can serve as a catalyst for one of these types of behavior from your romantic interest.

Essentially, we all have expectations for ourselves and of one another. When these expectations aren't met or are only partially met, it is a natural response for us to take this as a reflection on ourselves and our value as a whole. Although not the most preferred response, this can be beneficial if used objectively (for example, asking ourselves what we could've done to improve the outcome). But—as we've all seen first-hand—keeping our emotions in check isn't as easy as it sounds. And so, failing to meet an expectation damages our emotional well-being more often than not.

The causes of failed expectations can come in a variety of scenarios. But these would be the general underlying factors:

- Wanting what we can't have
- Settling for what we don't want
- Getting less than we desire (or feel we deserve)

In today's society, it's rather commonplace to compare ourselves to others and ask ourselves questions such as, "Why can't I have what they have?" and "Am I not good enough for that?" This desire to use others as the base of reference for what could be made available to us does far more harm than good as we not only tend to find greater cause for complaint than gratitude, but we also begin to assume that having anything less than that immediately reflects negatively on us as individuals. We want that car, that house, that following on social media, that job, that man (or someone just like him), etc. And the more we think about it, the more unfair it feels that we seemingly have less to show for ourselves; especially if we feel we've worked just as hard or harder for that level of success and happiness.

Again, we come into a place of attaching self-worth to the achievement of our desires (or surpassing someone else's achievements). We want something tangible to show for ourselves and for others to see and acknowledge. But this way of thinking doesn't serve us in the least. It only breeds jealousy and envy. And these are not the kinds of experiences that God wants us to have. We've probably all heard this before, but it truly is what is on the inside that counts. And there is no greater thing or experience outside of ourselves. Our greatest experience is the experience of peace, harmony, gratitude, and love; the experience that we feel when we commune with God. Through that alone anything is possible. But what happens when we let our disappointments get the best of us? What happens when we look outside of ourselves and only see lack? Many studies on the subconscious suggest that because it works diligently to establish a sense of normal, every bit of feedback we receive is helping to either reinforce or reestablish our sense of normal. So, it shouldn't seem too unreasonable to assume that our fears would start to show to others in a multitude of undesirable ways.

When the fear of not receiving what we crave emotionally becomes strong enough to influence your behavior (or the behavior of another) it is not uncommon to see any of these fear-based characteristics begin to play a role in your approach to relationships with others:

- Dominance
    - Controlling (and possibly even abusive) behavior
    - Cold-heartedness towards to needs and desires of others (especially when it runs the risk of compromising what you want)
    - Stubbornness toward concepts presented by others (especially the one you are in a romantic relationship with)
- Insecurity
    - Low self-esteem
    - Accepting of consistent (sometimes egregious) mistreatment from their partner
    - People pleaser
    - Clingy behavior to the point of desperation
    - Jealousy
- Selfishness
    - Self-centered behavior
    - Unwilling to change or go out of their way for others at the risk of getting less for themselves
    - Entitled; often convinced that they deserve more than they normally receive
- Infidelity
    - A pleasure seeker that feels they aren't getting

enough of what they want from what they have
- ○ Tired of asking (or feeling like they always have to ask) for what they want from their partner. So, they begin looking for it in situations/scenarios where it comes more naturally
- Victimization
    - ○ Feels that they generally get the short end of a situation
    - ○ This could lead them to react more selfishly at times or to become accustomed to exceedingly self-sacrificing behavior to a fault such as settling for a partner or relationship that continually hinders their personal growth and/or happiness

As you can see, there are a handful of ways that a lacking emotional foundation can lead to a fear-based reaction in relationships. Fear of what you ask? Fear of never receiving the type of love you've always yearned for. Fear of never finding affirmation that you are just as worthy of unconditional love as every other person who receives it. Fear that you'll be forced to settle with an emptiness inside that no one will ever want to fill.

In their own right, these are valid fears. We all probably know of a few people who never seemed to find love or who seemed to be living a life filled with depression, disappointment, and regret as their time winds down. But again, let us encourage you to keep in mind that not everyone is 'doomed' to experience the same mistakes and disappointments as their ancestors.

In a similar fashion, tradition has imbued a metaphorical shackling on our mind which can be exemplified in some of the terms used to describe our romantic partner; and thereby reflect our opinion of ourselves in the relationship or as a whole. Phrases such as 'ball and chain' or 'my better half' suggest that your partner is either a great hindrance to you or your only redeeming factor. In either of these cases, one of you is being put down; which potentially reflects negatively on the both of you.

To consider someone a great hindrance would suggest that you may be too weak-willed, lazy, or undesirable (in one or more ways) to find a suitable companion for yourself. Conversely, referring to your romantic partner as the better part of you suggest not only that you aren't a whole person, but also that you are the lesser of your relationship's sum total. This not only reflects poorly on you, but also places your partner in that same role of the person who is settling for less than they deserve by remaining with you.

If you've been using phrases like these to describe your significant other, we would like to take this opportunity to invite you to reframe this particular habit of speech. It may seem unimportant but we the scriptures say that 'life and death is in the power of the tongue' so we shouldn't take that lightly.

At this point, we would imagine that reading all this might already have you not feeling so great about the fact that you have one or more of the detrimental habits we've mentioned. But know that, as long as you live and breathe, you have time to reflect and change for the better. And if you start by acknowledging the type of love that most strongly resonates with you, you will be on your way to uncovering where things started to break down for you and how you can repair them by allowing God to mold you into the whole person you were created to be. You don't need anything or anyone (outside of God) to validate your worth. You will understand how perfect God's design is when you learn to cherish the unconditional love that He has for you.

And so, without any further ado, we will present the four spiritual pillars of whole love. Feel free to read through these a couple of times and as yourself which pillar most powerfully communicates an undeniable love to you when shown by others.

The Four Spiritual Pillars of Whole Love

PRESENCE - In as much as you value being in the presence of the Lord, having someone you value share their time with you can go a long way to communicate that you are worth the time. When you think of that comforting feeling of security, protection, and communion with God, you think of Him being present in that space with you. By providing your presence to others, you should also be present; meaning you aren't thinking about some past or future events. You are focused only on your time in that present moment with the person or people you are there for. For only that is true presence.

Loving Touch - We think of the hand of God as a loving hand. But in an effort not to misconstrue the types of physical touch that one can use as a means of hiding feelings, this touch is rooted deeply in love and loving energy. There are some who feel awkward or afraid of saying things like, "I love you." In these instances, it isn't uncommon for someone to use a punch to the arm to express fond feelings. Others may use touch in a sexual or lustful manner; resorting to more intimate contact as their means of showing affection or interest. But that can easily be misinterpreted from feelings of lust, since lust derives from selfish desire. Loving touch—which can include pats on the back, hugs and kisses, etc.—would be some of the ways we might imagine God would show His unyielding love for you if He were right in front of you in the flesh.

Offerings - These would be gifts of a more spiritual nature. When you think of what fills and sustains the church. The resources that we give as a token communion, it would be through offerings. But there is a greater offering, one that sustains our salvation today, which is the sacrifice of Christ's life on the cross. Offerings should be understood as sacrifices willingly given up or offered for another's sake—without necessarily expecting anything in return.

Verbal Unification - This is to affirm that there is a sense of harmony and accordance between what is and what should be through your words. Another way of putting this is saying that you are pleased with what is simply because it is (this may sound strange). But more simply put, it means that you positively acknowledge someone else in the same way that you would appreciate being acknowledged yourself. Think of the saying, do unto others. If we are truly unified, wouldn't it also make sense to speak unto others as you would have spoken unto yourself? Say the constructive, appreciative things that you would like for someone else to say to you. As you build others up, you will both indirectly and directly build yourself up as praise and encouragement are vital for developing a healthy psyche.

To better illustrate our point, and help recognize the signs and symptoms of brokenness, we'll be following the stories of four characters throughout this book (Dana, Brittany, Meghan, and Rhonda). Through the examples provided in their stories, our hope is that you will be able to better identify some likenesses within yourself and others so that your approach is not only gentle and forgiving, but also accurate and effective.

That said, you may not be an exact match to any of these stories. You may only find pieces of what describe you or other people. If that is the case, use these examples to the best of your ability and connect the dots to gain a better understanding of where you may be in need of more self-healing and tough love, if necessary.

Four Broken Lovers

Character 1: Dana

DANA GREW UP IN A HOME with parents who weren't big on things like hugs and kisses or positive verbal feedback. In school, she knew what was expected of her, as well as the consequences (such as being grounded or having something she really liked taken away) for failing to meet her parents' expectations. Whenever she met or exceeded expectations, her parents might take her out for dinner or allow her to have an additional scoop of ice cream for dessert. Rarely did she receive any words of encouragement during her struggles or smaller successes. So, she mostly only came to expect a response when something either went really well or really poorly.

By the time she was in college, Dana started to experience more of the physical touch she craved from the boys who were interested in her. And without the restrictions of her parents to prevent her from being out late or exploring intimacy it wasn't long before she had gone through multiple relationships with multiple guys. But the majority of them were short lived, leaving her feeling inadequate and envious of those of her friends with better romantic relationships than hers.

Her fear of being abandoned and ignored was expressed through angry outbursts and clingy behavior that only served to drive men away all the faster. Some men even began to avoid her after hearing stories from their friends about how crazy and jealous she could be. And whenever she did meet a guy who she expected to have heard those rumors about her, she was quick to try and make them feel like everyone else had it out for her. Eventually, even those situations went awry as each guy came to understand why the rumors existed in the first place.

If any of her friends tried to intervene or offer advice on how she could improve the way she came off to others, she was quick to defend herself and say that they were taking everyone else's side. In some instances, she had a falling out with one or more friends over these types of conversations; which she viewed as personal attacks.

By the end of her college years, she could count her friends on one hand. And no matter how many singles parties, holy ghost hookups, or dating apps she tried, Dana had even worse luck with finding a good man to settle down with since none of them were willing to settle for her.

Character 2: Brittany

BRITTANY WAS THE TYPE of child that had most anything and everything she could've wanted. Both of her parents were well-paid professionals, but at the cost of holding down occupations with long and demanding hours. It was commonplace for them to have a babysitter or relative taking care of her after school. Sometimes they came home so late it was up to her to make her own dinner.

By the time she was in middle school, she was old enough to take care of herself. And that's exactly what she did. Up until the end of her college years, Brittany had become rather used to not seeing her parents on any given day. But because she had learned to be self-sufficient, it hardly bothered her by this point.

In terms of romantic relationships, she would often give her best effort and, in some cases, she seemed overly excited about the relationship before she even knew the guy she was dating all that well. Because Brittany often had such high hopes for relationships, she found it easy to ignore obvious issues early on. But, it never took long before she found herself keeping a tally on the number of times she felt let down by each guy. And it was never long before she started to have doubts about each relationship and whether or not it had much of a future.

Some of her friendships had a similar tone. But because she had higher expectations for each guy that could be the one, even her best romantic relationships tended to have a significantly shorter lifespan than some of her weakest friendships. It wasn't hard for her friends to notice her dilemma, and on more than one occasion, they recommended that she stop trying to find the perfect man, and place more focus on finding a good man that did his best to keep her happy.

But at some stage in her life, Brittany came to an even greater turning point. And in an effort to prevent herself from being alone at every friend or relative's wedding or special event, she came to the conclusion that she would have to stop being so picky. So, she started accepting more and more of what she didn't want in relationships for the sake of remaining in a relationship. She told herself that she was seeing the bigger picture and that because no relationship was perfect, she would have to be more reasonable about compromising on the little things.

Unfortunately, in her current relationship, she's come across so many little things that she feels trapped between her desire to not be alone and her yearning to find a lasting sense of happiness with someone she can honestly say that she loves and is in love with. She doesn't know what to do. The relationship has become so toxic that the same friends who were once encouraging her to stop looking for the perfect man are telling her she needs to aim higher. They encourage her to focus on finding someone who truly appreciates her and is genuinely a good fit for her.

Character 3: Meghan

MEGHAN WAS THE KIND of kid who craved attention and making friends. Because she was artsy, she often created all kinds of imaginative drawings and paintings and showed her parents or her older brother; hoping not only for encouragement, but also to convince them of how fun it was. Best-case scenario, they would accept her regular invitations to create art with her. Worst-case, they might at least get her more of the art supplies she asked for most every Christmas or birthday. In her mind, if she could prove that she was making the best of what she had, it was only a matter of time before someone took notice and thought to contribute to her cause and propel her to greater heights.

But as time went on, she didn't find that many people supporting her artistic pursuits. And the older she got, the more she lost hope in others to come to her aid in what she felt should've been a trivial matter for them. By the time she entered college, she'd decided to focus on a major that could provide a solid income, even if she didn't enjoy it. She believed that the promise of self-sustaining income would be enjoyable in its own way because with money she would have more opportunities. More importantly, she believed it would allow her to fund her dreams without the need of others.

By the end of college, she had her business degree and was working in a career that paid well, but wasn't very rewarding in any other way. Even though she was able to buy whatever she wanted to fuel her artistic pursuits, and even though she had her own house, and little to no financial obligations whatsoever, she couldn't help feeling like something was missing. Meghan hoped that her feelings could be resolved by finding the right man, but no matter what she did or how hard she tried to keep them happy, the relationships never lasted. It was as if no man could appreciate her sacrifices for them.

The most recent guy she met seemed like a change of pace from the others. He often told her how amazing she was and how much he enjoyed being with her. He regularly complimented her efforts to stay in shape and make sure that he always had a warm meal when he came home from work; even though her job was equally demanding. It finally felt like all of her hard work was paying off and someone was taking notice. But, when Meghan was approached for a promotion that would require so much of her time that she would have to cut something out of her life, she became anxious. hardly hesitated before choosing art as the thing to be cut out.

She didn't want to risk the promotion souring her relationship, so she sought his approval before accepting. At first, he seemed accepting and happy for Meghan. But within six months of accepting her promotion, her love life had taken a turn for the worst. Her new role was so demanding, she found herself working more hours than originally expected. And ever since she took on her new position, her greatest focus became doing everything in her power to keep from letting her boss and co-workers down.

Before long, the same man who once admired her for how hard she worked decided he'd had enough. After a long day of work, she came home to meet with a frustrated man and his ultimatum. He said he didn't like her working long hours or not having time to cook for him anymore. And even though she'd willingly given up on practicing art ever since she took on the new role, she still couldn't make the time to make sure he was happy. So, it was the job or him, and she had to choose.

Character 4: Rhonda

RHONDA GREW UP AS THE middle child of five. And because her father was almost completely out of the picture ever since the age of seven, everything seemed to be in short supply for her. No matter how well she did in school or how much she went out of her way to help around the house, she didn't seem to get half the attention of her older or younger siblings. Bringing home A's on her report card or getting top scores in her class were hardly met with any more than a 'good job' or a pat on the head. It was a frustrating and emotionally lacking experience for her, and the older she got, the more she sought something more fulfilling.

In high school, she was valedictorian, and had it not been for her principal reaching out to her mother to remind her about the graduation and let them know how proud and excited she was about Rhonda's upcoming valedictorian speech during graduation, her mother wouldn't even have known about it. This alarmed her mom, and when confronted about why she didn't let her know about the graduation or about her speech, she said, "It must've slipped my mind. But that's okay. It's no big deal." This was only one example of how independent and even distant she had become with daily life.

By college, Rhonda was the type of person that not only preferred to live her life without any authoritative input, she nearly craved it. Even among friends, she was known as the responsible one, and she often didn't like to give that role over to anyone else.

Her relationships with men seemed to go well at first. But she never made it to a full year with any guy. At some point, the relationships always got to her, and whenever she came into disappointment from the guy's actions or confrontations about any disagreements, she repeatedly distanced herself from them until they gave up and ended the relationship.

Because she started to see more and more of the same thing from every guy, she began to wonder if serious relationships were meant for her at all, and eventually turned to serial dating with multiple guys at a time. She never let any of them get too close, and if she couldn't get the intimacy she wanted from one, she would go to another guy for it. This continued for some number of years. But as she sees how happy all of her friends are in their relationships, she is once again at a crossroads. Wishing she either had something just as good as what they had or that they didn't have anything at all, so she wouldn't have to feel like she was the problem.

Summary

IT'S NOT A RARE INSTANCE by any measure to find that you exhibit one or more behaviors that show that you're broken. It's far more common that many of us go through much of our lives not realizing that we are broken or just how broken we are. But as long as you understand which pillars of whole love most deeply resonate as your proof of love, you can begin to uncover where in your life you feel that those pillars are lacking. And with that knowledge you can take those necessary first steps toward determining not only which broken behaviors you tend to resort to as a cry for help, but more importantly, you can learn how to resolve these issues and become a whole person.

The four spiritual pillars of whole love are:

- Presence
  - Being present with others; meaning that you aren't thinking about some past or future events. You are focused only on sharing your time in that present moment with the person or people you are there for.
- Loving Touch
  - Can include pats on the back, hugs and kisses, etc.—would be some of the ways we might imagine God would show His unyielding love for you if He were right in front of you in the form of man.
- Offerings
  - Making a willing sacrifice (of time, energy, etc.) for another's sake—without necessarily expecting something in return.
- Verbal Unification

- ° Positively acknowledging something that is agreeable in someone else in the same way that you would appreciate something within yourself.

Chapter 2: Roots of Brokenness

———

First Impressions are Everything

As an infant, all you were able to bring to the table of a relationship was your needs. Your need to be loved, held, fed, wrapped in a bandage and kissed over your knee when you fell and got a boo boo. As a little girl, all you needed was an overly exaggerated 'WOW' after telling your parents, "Look what I did," as a means of reaffirming your worth.

But when your needs are encountered by the very same parents whose needs have gone unmet since they were your age, a cycle begins. Due to the turbulent and overwhelming nature of adulthood, your parents may have been too under equipped to satisfy your basic emotional and mental needs. This great need clashing with a parent's emotional incompetence may have created enduring internal conflicts for you, even if your parents intended on loving you well.

More likely than not your parents were reared in a household where a healthy means of expressing love was rarely—if ever—properly exampled. As a result of this ignorance, you've become the casualty of someone else's brokenness. An ancestral brokenness that is passed down through generations. Your parents ended up as bigger broken children, reproducing smaller ones. You all have been piling the shards of yourselves into clusters and calling it a family. We must be able to recognize and grow past this vicious cycle. Together we will uncover the issues that drove us to ground zero so that we can greatly improve our chances of resolving this generational brokenness once and for all. And it all starts with YOU.

Our Two-Fold Existence

GOD HAS CREATED HUMAN beings—complex in many ways, but there is a simple yet profound TWO-FOLD nature that we believe He's programmed for us. That nature is what governs our existence. God has given all living things (people especially) the ability to receive and give; to be poured into and to pour out. Plants, through the process of photosynthesis are beautiful in the way that they take in carbon dioxide and sunlight energy and, in turn, produce oxygen; helping other organisms breathe. We share this quality with plants and every other living organism, but in a much more interesting way.

The first fold of our nature deals with our natural ability to receive and be shaped. All the experiences we have good and bad, shape us in one way or another, our world outlook is based on these factors. Because early childhood is our most important time of being molded, the first fold of our nature is most impacted during this stage. Out first fold is what determines *identity*.

The second fold our nature deals with our instinctive desire to give of ourselves. While our basic physical human tendencies are more bent on surviving for self, our inner being is driven by a greater call. There is a distinct satisfaction that comes from doing for others. Being able to bless, encourage and love others fulfills a deeper part of us. The part of us that is stimulated most by selfless endeavors is tied to our souls. We believe this is our *God consciousness*. It's the trait that reminds us we are made in the image of God. This fold propels us towards the apex of our purpose.

Human beings can never reach a level of a wholeness unless they are able to reconcile and heal our capacity for both folds of existence, identity and purpose.

Don't Dismiss Spiritual Warfare

WE WANT TO BE CLEAR that it's unhealthy to blame all dysfunction on the devil and demons. Even though I (Ezekiel) was raised in a hyper spiritual Nigerian culture where we would call down fire, thunder and heavenly machine guns, it may not be a fix all remedy for every issue we encounter. Sometimes people have mental health issues. Other times, the flaws in humanity rear its ugly head in the lives of some more than others. However, we don't want to diminish the unseen battles that we are facing as believers. Scripture tells us in Ephesians 6:12:

> *"For we wrestle not against flesh and blood, but against principalities, against powers, against the rulers of the darkness of this world, against spiritual wickedness in high places."*

Clearly all we endure within our lives can't be boxed into simple happenstances of living. We are at war. The enemy loves to use people and circumstances to destroy what God intends to do in us.

In Mark Chapter 9, Jesus is confronted by a father who desperately wants his child healed from a demon that plagues him. The father describes how this spirit would manifest and cause his son to hurt himself by falling in fire and water to "destroy him." Although this instance of scripture is more of an ode to the power of Christ and the importance of prayer. It's vital to see how the kingdom of darkness works hand in hand with our early conflict and trauma to destroy us when we are young. Jesus asked how long had he dealt with the issue, and the father replies, "since he was a child". We must learn to pray diligently for our children and the younger generation around us. The enemy is working overtime to undermine God's work in children, who will grow up to be leaders and changers in our world for Christ.

The scriptures tell us that the enemy comes to steal, kill and destroy. We sincerely don't believe that the enemy is truly satisfied until he's able to do all three in our lives. We're inclined to believe that Satan approaches progressively. He may start by stealing so that he may kill, then eventually destroy. Simply causing you to get traffic tickets, making you late for work, and giving you a bad hair day can't be the true work of the enemy. If he can successfully steal your early days, he becomes more prepared to kill your present days, so when it's all said and done he can finally destroy your future. But today, we say the devil is a liar! We know that the enemy is ultimately after our second fold of existence; our purpose. This is the reason he goes after the first fold of our existence; our identity. If the enemy can corrupt what shapes us, he can also dictate how we shape the world around us.

But with the insight we gain from this book and the power of the Spirit within us, our purpose will be realized and revived in Jesus' name!

Complex Trauma

THROUGHOUT THIS AND the next chapter you will continue to see the use of the word trauma. Too often we associate trauma with devastating major events that harmfully affect the psyche. However, complex trauma can be a bit subtler. Though some instances of complex trauma can be devastating, it's the repetition and the time period of this trauma that makes it so difficult to overcome. When an infant or child experiences the breakdown of their first fold of existence, and love is not properly being poured into them, it affects them in significant ways. The trauma we will spend most time dealing with is the type that results from cumulative experiences that have negatively impacted us overtime.

It Is a Big Deal

IF WE TAKE THE SEED for granted, the tree will be unconquerable. If we don't recognize the small errors, we will never understand how they grew into the big monsters of dysfunction that we are currently seeing and experiencing.

Numbness Isn't Healing.

JUST BECAUSE YOU SEEMINGLY have been able to succeed in various facets of life doesn't mean that you've effectively identified, confronted, or resolved your traumatic experiences. You will see, as we continue to work through this, that many behaviors don't just develop from a whim. Some of our actions are simply reactions to seeds of complex trauma that have conditioned our behavior into survival strategies.

Freezing at Trauma

BY NOW, YOU MAY BE thinking, "I'm a grown woman!" Is it truly possible that im exhibiting behaviors triggered from childhood issues?"

Absolutely! In fact, the majority of our adult perspectives have been entirely shaped by our upbringing; both good and bad. The significant characteristic of trauma in the development of a child is that it has the tendency to freeze your development at whatever stage you were in when the trauma occurred. There are forty, fifty, and sixty-year-olds alike (many of whom we know personally) who seem to have character flaws that can only be associated with the outer workings of a bad child. We may not be too far off with that diagnosis. It's possible that the individuals you're thinking about are acting out as a result of being psychologically frozen at that stage of their trauma. While they have the ability to mature in other facets of their lives, there still may be areas they have progressed no further than that of a seven or eight-year-old child. We must be empathetic in these cases because we may have more in common with them than we thought.

Surviving Trauma

I REMEMBER WHEN I (Ezekiel) tried to be Superman. Early on in my relationship with Kiyanna I noticed a bit of tension and hostility from Kiyanna to her biological father. I wasn't used to such things because I grew up with both parents married and in the home. She would tell me she's doing the best she could and she's still working on processing the residue of bitterness left behind by him not being a part of her life early on. I was tragically confused. I would ask how could she hold such a grudge after all these years? So I set up an appointment (without her permission) for them to squash the beef in ten minutes. It was a disaster. She was pregnant with our first child and was forced to deal with the stress of holding a little human in her belly and the stress of unraveling her heart on a platter within a few moments. Needless to say, they needed a bit more time, communication and understanding for the healing to stick.

We've all probably had someone tell us to 'get over it'. But it's not that simple. It takes will and intentionality to move past the shadows of our deepest wounds. Our minds have the ability to temporarily suppress unfavorable thoughts and feelings in order to continue functioning as we have been. Our bodies naturally rank the actions we take with a sense of survival-based priority. And after the essentials for survival (such as food, water, shelter, and sanitation) are taken care of, our focus quickly shifts over to comfort. When comfort is at the forefront of our focus, emotional effort (such as processing painful thoughts) can go completely ignored for as long as we can convince ourselves that the investment of time or energy is too great. Even if we viewed this as a necessity in some sense, tasks such as locating food, maintaining our shelter, and earning a living will always outrank our efforts toward personal growth. In other words, it takes high emotional intelligence to realize that healing past mental trauma matters more than eating, hanging out with friends, or binge-watching an entire season of our favorite television shows over the course of a single weekend (and don't think for a second that only watching half of that season makes you any better).

Let's be clear in our understanding, personal growth is not a means to survive, but rather a means to thrive. Your body as is, can give you signs but will never lead you towards wholeness. Because the body follows our direction and is not concerned with our tomorrow, but tends to only assists us with making it through the day. And that simple truth allows us to trick ourselves into feeling temporary moments of normalcy; as if all is well with both us and the world around us. But do not be fooled. At the very best, all we are truly experiencing is a consistent suppression of critical issues. Constant denial of truth conditions us to become content with our brokenness. The brain is deprioritizing its own mental solidarity and health for the sake of survival but you must quickly regain control of yourself before you survive, to death.

Think about it. Is surviving actually living? For many of us, it's the only state of existence we've known. By definition, to survive simply communicates, 'not dead'. Although not being dead is reason for gratitude, it is by no means the same as living in the fullness that God has created for us; His beloved children that He sacrificed so much for.

> "Beloved, I pray that in all respects you may prosper and be in good health, just as your soul prospers"
>
> 3 John 1:2
>
> "...I came so everyone would have life, and have it fully."
>
> John 10:10

It's clear to see that Christ came that we may experience life fully and wholly; instead of merely surviving in the way that we had before Him. We were made to prosper. As believers, it is our re-birthright. But prosperity extends far beyond financial stability. It includes physical, mental and emotional soundness. It is the very same harmony that exists within the Trinity itself.

So, what does surviving trauma look like day to day? We all know of Darwin's "theory" of evolution and how it unsuccessfully attempts to debunk creationism. We can't completely invalidate all parts of that theory. We believe that there is a smidge of truth within his concept. Darwin's theory of evolution claimed that all living organisms evolved from one simple organism but, over time, those organisms continually adapted to both favorable and unfavorable environments in order to survive. It conveyed that organisms shed traits that didn't help and overtime developed traits that increased chances for survival.

A few billion years later, random selection and adaptation have collectively facilitated the millions of species on planet earth today.

However, unlike surviving harsh climates or droughts, trauma doesn't necessarily make us better people. More often than not, it tricks us into thinking we are okay if we can find a temporary means of escaping the pain.

Emotional Chemotherapy

HUMANS HAVE A NATURAL tendency of resisting unfavorable circumstances by creating ways to deflect them at all costs. Think about the human body. When the body is hit with an illness, the white blood cells go on attack mode to fight the infection and communicates with the rest of the immune system to better prevent it from happening again. This is the healthy way the body fights sickness.

But what happens when the sickness is too great for the body to handle alone? Take cancer for example, it's one of the leading causes of death in today's society. Modern medicine's best approach to combating this issue is a man-made means of destroying those pesky cancerous cells; chemotherapy.

The process of chemotherapy has proven to be an effective treatment for many. In some cases, it functions as a vital treatment to sustain the lives of those afflicted with more severe categories of cancer. Many people all over the world (including our loved ones) have benefited from chemotherapy. But we do want to address the volatility of such a process so that we can properly shed light on the concept of *Emotional Chemotherapy*. Chemotherapy uses medication to kill cells; and while it aims for the bad, it unfortunately will terminate a lot of good cells in the process. It would be similar to a blindfolded civilian running into an elementary school with an automatic rifle and firing to kill a group of terrorists who've taken the school hostage. Such an uncalculated approach would inevitably lead to numerous unwanted casualties. So, even if the cause of the problem is snuffed out, it would be at the cost of the lives of the very hostages whose lives were meant to be saved. What we're referring to as emotional chemotherapy is another way of describing how we attempt to protect ourselves from being hurt again. Trying to simply distance ourselves from our problems or dismiss them as unworthy of our attention is more reckless than many of us realize. And yet we learn from others (both directly and indirectly) that it is an accepted and—at times—even recommended response to emotional pain. When our approach toward our issues is either blindly aggressive or passive, we hurt ourselves and everyone in our path.

Absenteeism of One or Both Parents

The loss of either or both parents is convincingly devastating for a child's development. The trauma attached to an absentee parent can turn children into what we would consider the troubled individuals of our communities.

As daughters, we have the habit of interpreting a parent's absence as a direct indictment on our value. The fact that dad didn't care enough to stay or mom gave us up at birth means we are not wanted like other children are. This doubt of self-worth can manifest in many different ways that are harmful to us as children and as we transition into womanhood. A lack of self-love or a low view of self can prove detrimental not just to us but all potential relationships we may attempt to build. Because once this trauma has been inflicted we can spend our lives exhibiting behaviors that are really anesthetics. We become experts at numbing the pain. Maneuvering to escape every path that may lead us to the original agony attached to the trauma.

Despite how your parents did not show up in your life, it's your job to identify areas in your life where you're attempting to fill the void of their presence. Are you quick to anger? Maybe your anger is an outward expression of a deeper sadness within, and you're wearing anger as a mask and lashing out at others not realizing that your wound was inflicted by feelings of abandonment. These feelings have made you feel unworthy of love that you indeed deserved from your parents. We want you to know that it's not your fault. Despite the circumstances that shaped you, your parents' shortcomings do not have to determine your potential. Instead you can use your understanding of this void to seek out others who may be going through something similar and pour into them.

Face this loss, but don't own the blame. Your healing begins at knowing that your trauma is not your destiny. It may seem strange, but because you know what it's like to endure this trauma you have the ability to show others better ways to cope with it.

When the Pillars of Whole Love Collapse

PILLARS ARE THE FOUNDATIONAL beams that keep structures from toppling over and being reduced to debris. As chapter one mentioned, the pillars of love are our proofs of love. Without the pillars of Presence, Offerings, Loving Touch and Verbal Unification, you may have grown up feeling you were not loved enough or loved at all. It's not just about hearing "I love you", there are intentional demonstrations of love that your parents should have shown to reinforce a healthy psyche for you.

Lack of Presence

THE FINAL PICTURE IS in its place, the camera must've flashed almost as bright as the smiles on this family, all wearing their Sunday best. It's a beautiful family photo album. Brittany flips through the pages with half a smirk on her face. She's definitely proud of her work. She stares at an old photo of her and her parents propped up on their living room couch. "I look just like my mom, and my dad", she thinks to herself. Despite such extensive memories, the only emotion she had while completing this family album for her school project was fear. Fear that she wouldn't be able to complete it on time. In her mind it was just another project. The only difference was that this one was supposed to be a project that the whole family was supposed to work on with her. She knows in advance that the idea of cooperating amongst strangers is a fantasy at best. She doesn't remember the last time she's had a meaningful conversation with either one of her parents. Sometimes mom asks "how's school?" while on hold on a phone call but Brittany knows she's asking just because she thinks it's the motherly thing to do. Her call would resume midway through Brittany's answer and she'd raise that one index finger that meant goodbye for now and later. Dad was no better, sometimes she felt that if his laptop had a left hand, he would put a ring on it. Often times days would go by before she saw his face emerge from his digital stock market world. Brittany is jaded by the idea of family but she's becoming desperate for someone to be there with her and for her, no matter what it costs.

Just because they were there, doesn't mean they were there.

On the surface the two phrases seem to be the same, but when you look at the lives of women who have experienced true presence from their parents, and compare them to those who haven't, the difference is night and day.

The pillar of Presence is not just the physical location of the body but an intentional focus and engagement with an object of affection, in this case, you. A young girl who receives consistent intentional and focused time from her father is more likely to have higher self-esteem and generally better behavior. Presence communicates to a young lady's mind that she is special enough to be paid attention to. It tells her that her dreams and concerns are worth hearing. A little girl in you has this innate need for security, and daddy doesn't need to be super tall with big muscles to provide that. His reassuring voice, his calm temperament and leadership all settle your heart with serenity. A girl that grows up with a positive father present is less likely to fall prey to just any joker on the street with a good pick up line. She has seen the necessary sacrifice and effort her father has invested into her family and wouldn't be as easily *played* as the next girl. Without her father, she is more likely to swing towards extreme spectrums of emotional imbalance, and have difficulties relating romantically to men in the future.

Sometimes I (Kiyanna) think of all the ups and downs I've had in my relationship with my mother. I look at all of her hard work and sacrifices she made for me and my siblings when we were children and soak in gratitude. However, my fondest memories with her are those that we spent alone. Times when I used to feel insecure about being the darkest child in the house. She would take time to show me magazines of beautiful dark-skinned women and remind me that I was beautifully and wonderfully made. We didn't have as many of these moments that I would have wanted but these are moments that keep me confident today and preserve our relationship when things get shaky. I also feel it is a lack of those intentional focused conversations and time spent that create our current disconnect. Maybe we would understand each other even more and get along as well as we both desire to, if true presence was made a priority. A mother's presence is so impactful for a young girl's emotional development. You would not only be able to mirror healthy character traits, but your dormant abilities would have bloomed, allowing you to become a source of nurture and care in the home. This time spent communicates to you as a daughter that you are loved, and worthy of being cared for and catered to. Young girls that receive this presence from mothers with healthy discipline in place are more fluent in empathy and consideration.

Lack of intentional time and energy given willingly from either parent can drive a woman towards troubled relationships in the future. When you discover that you're clingy or even obsessive in relationships, you may be reaping a lack of quality presence. Are you struggling with self-discipline? Are there addictions you're dealing with that you're ashamed of? Do people consider you insensitive or cold hearted? These may also be symptoms of a lack of quality presence.

Lack of Loving Touch

RHONDA HASN'T GONE out to recess for two months. Once again she's sitting on Ms. Martinez's lap, the teacher's assistant. Once again they're reading another Dr. Seuss book. Ms. Martinez doesn't have any children of her own so she doesn't mind coddling Rhonda all the time. Mrs. Dawson (the lead teacher), finds it all quite strange. Rhonda's reading assessment places her at a 7th grade reading level while Dr. Seuss books cater to 1st graders. Rhonda even curls up into Ms. Martinez and pretends to struggle through the rhyming lines when they are together. Mrs. Dawson has already mentioned this issue during a parent conference but her parents believe it's just a phase. Rhonda desires physical touch from her parents but her dad is out of the picture and mom has never been affectionate towards her children. Rhonda makes the most of her time with Ms. Martinez, and doesn't know that this void will be taking her down a path that will cause her to hunt for love through physical contact at her own detriment.

Think back, how often did your parents hug you, kiss you, rub your back while watching tv, touch your knee during a conversation or even caress your face? If this sounds foreign to you then you may currently be uncomfortable with most forms of affection through touch or have experienced a lingering void of a lack of love that has wreaked havoc on your self-esteem.

Unfortunately, as we discussed in chapter one it's hard to mention physical touch without allowing perverted concepts to bombard our brains. Why? Because it happens. There are people in this world; some that unfortunately end up in our families, that misuse their access to loved ones to cause pain and brokenness. (we will save this for later). What we want to talk about is why our parents didn't give us enough of these loving touches? Before we proceed, it's important that we not use our understanding of these ideas to prosecute our parents for their shortcomings. In most cases, parents love their children dearly but often are not equipped to love them in ways that are most effective for healthy development. The tools we are gathering now are to help heal ourselves and prevent pain for generations to come.

Our parents may not have recognized the value of the pillars of whole love, and certainly did not realize the power of loving physical gestures on their daughters.

This idea of a loving touch didn't spawn from thin air. Throughout scripture there is mention of Jesus touching people to heal them. It's safe to say that the Son of God could have found a way to heal people that required no contact at all. The simple fact that He touched communicated his desire for showing that his healing was an expression of his love for them.

> *"People were also bringing babies to Jesus for him to place his hands on them. When the disciples saw this, they rebuked them. But Jesus called the children to him and said, 'Let the little children come to me, and do not hinder them, for the kingdom of God belongs to such as these.'*

This passage in Luke 18:15-16 beautifully describes Jesus rebuking others from keeping children from his loving hands, instead he calls them to come. Isn't that what a loving touch communicates? "I'm a safe place, come to me, be with me, I accept you." It's safe to say that living a life void of this consistent gesture can easily lead one to feel deep rejection and unwantedness. I (Kiyanna) didn't realize that Ezekiel was missing the pillar of loving touch growing up. His parents weren't the touchy type. West African culture didn't place high value on touching their kids with love; providing was more than enough. There would be times he would try to kiss me and it would catch me off guard so I would turn my face. Of course, I loved his kisses, but all affection outside of the bedroom used to make me feel dirty. I had no idea that he tied my actions to feelings of rejection. Me not allowing him to kiss me communicated to him, that I didn't believe he was attractive enough, or that I didn't want him as much as he wanted me. It devastated me that I participated in triggering mental and emotional damage that he carried over from childhood.

Lack of Verbal Unification

DANA HAS ANOTHER PARENT meeting today after school. This is the third time this semester and her parents have had it. All of Dana's teachers can attest to her proficiency in all subjects but for some reason, she keeps ending up in trouble. She hopscotches from anger tantrums in class to teasing other children during recess. Her parents don't understand how a third-grade child could be so disturbed when she comes from a decent two-parent household? They conclude it must be bad influences from peers or teachers failing her in the classroom. The root of Dana's acting out is right under their noses but they aren't willing to look inwardly for answers.

Remember the playground cliché 'sticks and stones may break my bones but words can never hurt me'? Well, that's a lie. The words that are composed about us or towards us have a significant impact on our view of ourselves and the world around us. In fact, the scriptures say,

"Death and life are in the power of the tongue" to emphasize the profound impact of the words we use towards others and words used towards us.

It's no exaggeration, the words that you have embraced about yourself are either contributing to your life or eating away at it, there is no middle ground.

Why verbal unification? When a couple is married, the reverend asks them to share vows of commitment to each other. After a deciding months ago that they want to be together forever, the vows during the ceremony are a testament of the decision. Family and friends become witnesses of those words to finalize the bond. Words spoken aloud, in a sense make concrete what could've only been assumed. Even our salvation weighs heavily on our confession of faith. Jesus completed the work on the cross but Romans 10:9-10 says:

"If you confess with your mouth and believe in your heart that Jesus was raised from the dead you shall be saved."

God in nature places so much weight on His word, the scripture even says He is His word. It makes so much sense that much is to be expected from us in relation to our words.

But how do words unify? Your parents loved you, and you felt like it was a given but could it have been that important for them to tell you? It was and still is. Many children grew up in homes where simple words of affection like 'I love you' were taboo. It seemed words of such vulnerability would undo their ability to function. Too many of our parents relied on us accepting the assumption that they loved us that they found it pointless to actually say it.

"I'm doing this because I love you." Imagine how comforted and energized you would feel as you moved through public settings after you heard those words at the top of your day. One simple "you're so beautiful or I'm proud of you" could've literally changed everything. Spiritually, positive reinforcement through words can bring you back to the heart of a relationship. These words help you desire to fight for the strength of a bond and against things that will threaten it. That's why we call it verbal unification, because they are words that not only keep a relationship together but have the power to keep you as a person together. However, many of us have been more accustomed to being riddled with vocabulary that dismantled us. How many times were you compared with other girls that were doing better in a particular area, or constantly under a hail of profanity. How often were you reminded of what you couldn't do, and how much you were missing the mark. These words said that you lacked value in the eyes of those who were supposed to love you. It forced you into a perpetual state of seeking our value from the words of others.

Lack of Offerings

MEGHAN SLOWLY WALKS down from the graduation stage to meet her parents. She saw them standing several feet away and her mother was holding those pink balloons again. Mom always went to the pharmacy to pick up pink balloons to celebrate Meghan for every occasion. Meghan drags her feet towards her with a fake smile. As she draws closer, her eyes pace around her parents to see if today would be different. She had written a few letters to Santa as well as her parents that included art she was proud of most. In the letters she wrote that all she wanted was an easel and a canvas. Her parents were hard-working middle-class people who felt they gave her everything she needed to be grateful, a roof over her head and clothes on her back. They never took her requests seriously and didn't think her art work was particularly special. They didn't realize that Meghan inwardly questioned their love for her because they weren't even willing to put the effort into getting her something that would've propelled her passion forward.

One of the most vivid pictures of love displayed is through the act of giving.

> *"For God so loved the world that He gave his only begotten son. Whosoever believes in him shall not perish, but have everlasting life."*

John 3:16

Along with the fact that this scripture is the foundation for the Gospel of Jesus Christ, it also allows us to see love come to life in a tangible way, God gave. That statement alone is sermon in and of itself. God's reasoning and motivation for giving such an inconvenient gift should leave us in awe. The bloody gift of his son on the cross is painfully, yet beautifully painted upon history's canvas. Understanding God's surrendering of His Son on the cross gives us a clearer picture of what offering truly looks like. He gave his *only* Son. This accentuates the idea that He did not render something replaceable. He did not give a spare. But even further, the way He gave Christ was through the death of crucifixion. Crucifixion was a grueling form of capital punishment perfected by Romans millenniums ago. In short, when God displayed his ultimate act of love, it cost him much.

> *"For it is by grace you have been saved, through faith—and this not from yourselves, it is the gift of God—not by works, so that no one can boast."*

Ephesians 2:8-9

This verse in Ephesians seems to contradict the idea that God gave such an expensive gift, how is it now that salvation is a gift that is presumably free.

This paradox is what makes the gift of Salvation the anchor of the way we should view this pillar of love. A true gift costs but is not deserved. If a gift is earned or deserved it becomes no more than wages for a duty. It's extremely special because we as mankind couldn't be saved in our power if we wanted to be, it's not something we can earn or work for. True Offerings in the form of service or tangible gift is unmerited just like the gift of salvation.

How often did we hear from our parents, 'clean your room and you'll get this', or 'eat your vegetables and you'll get this'? But while this can be a healthy practice that incentivizes children to cooperate, it's not a great example of a true offering.

We don't want to endorse the idea that parents should give children any and everything they want. Spoiling children in this fashion is harmful and can communicate a toxic form of entitlement that can follow them into adulthood. But it is no exaggeration to say that you may have measured the love of your parents by what was and wasn't given to you. And although you were immature in many ways, you were able to decipher true offerings from Cain offerings. You remember how Cain gave an offering that God wasn't pleased with? God asked Cain "If you would have given well, wouldn't you have been accepted?" Just like in Genesis, you can generally tell when a sacrifice is being made for you and when it isn't. Granted, there are some things parents don't get enough credit for, like supplying basic needs, clothes, food and shelter. While we do believe all children should be grateful for all the provisions parents make for them, providing essentials is one of the necessary mountains that parents should be expected to climb. You didn't bring yourself into this world, and children should, by default receive basic care from parents. Personalization of offerings make the difference. When you grow up in a family with multiple siblings, parents' attention is inevitably divided. The demand for personal love can exceed the supply, and often everyone is left with scraps. You went bananas during birthdays, why? Because finally you got a day specifically for you to be celebrated, to be thought about, sung for and given to simply because you were born. Gifts were given with your name on the box. Someone thought specifically about what you liked, and decided they would sacrifice money to get something for you that they hoped you would appreciate. But it didn't always have to be so grand, right? Sometimes it didn't require sacrificing money at all. Maybe an act of help would've been enough. It could've been as simple as mommy or daddy getting you dressed, helping you with your school project, or putting your bike together. Whether you've realized it or not, moments like this held significant meaning for you. The fact is they had a choice; one to do something for you, which benefited them in no way, or to do something for themselves that more than likely was more convenient. When they chose to give up the latter option and give you the former, they chose to render a true offering. And that sacrificial offering made you a better woman as a result. When your parents displayed acts of love through giving without expecting anything in return, it reinforced what was assumed, it substantiated what was hoped. True Offerings is the key ingredient to give solid evidence for what you as a child hoped and assumed about your parents, they truly loved you. But what happens when this hope isn't consistently reaffirmed? What happens when true unmerited gifts and help are seldom received? Some of us may attempt to earn love. Morph into people pleasers. People who are willing to sacrifice our peace of mind in an effort to earn the love of others.

Tumultuous Relationships

IT'S SAID THAT SECOND-hand smoke is just as bad as actually placing the cigarette to your lips and filling your lungs with the toxicity directly. You don't even have to be a smoker to wind up with lung cancer, how fair is that? Adults who get married seldom recognize the impact their union has on the healthy development of their child.

Once a child is brought into the picture, a marriage is no longer simply about two people getting together for a season, it's about laying a foundation that can last a generation.

Without even saying a word, when your parents have a healthy marriage, oceans of truth can submerge your mind. Your father loving your mother tells you that it's possible and noble to shower love upon the person who nurtures and feeds you. When your mother loves your father, it tells you that it's beautiful to submit and respond with love towards the person who protects and serves the family with honor. Your parents loving each other reminds you of the hope in commitment, romance and fidelity. It promises you that two different people, can endure the calamities of life and be victorious together. Your parents loving each other proves that the institution that God established years ago, still works, and is the most beautiful thing to see when it does.

Maybe your parents never saw eye to eye. Their heated arguments ironically had a way of making the home cold. They lived under the same roof, but were miserable, existing in a legal contract where both parties were dying to break out. Or maybe differences forced them to co parent, and you to choose sides. Your father down talking your mother when he had you for the weekend, or your mother was bashing him and his trifling ways whenever she got the chance. You would've rather they'd been strangers than two petty adults competing to see who could sling mud best.

Divorce

PERHAPS YOUR PARENTS decided one day that their differences were too great a mountain to climb, and you became a casualty of that tearing. When your home became a house, and your heart, a dark empty room. Divorce was a diagnosis that echoed throughout your childhood, and still hasn't let up its ring. In a war where there was no winner, your parents stood ten feet apart with pistols aimed at each other. Both unloaded their clips, with you standing in the middle of it all. It is by the grace of God you can live to tell about the wounds that made you a living testimony. Few can truly console the trauma inflicted from a bitter divorce, all you know is that you refuse to allow it to ever happen to you.

Abuse

YOU MAY HAVE BEEN A witness to vivid verbal or even physical abuse. Often times it was a man in the home that unleashed his anger on your mother, or even upon you and your siblings. Maybe it was sexual abuse from someone you trusted. The fear birthed from that type of terror isn't easy to shake. You may be reading this and the horror of what you witnessed and endured in your home has caused you to emotionally flee from the potential of this atmosphere. Unknowingly, your behavior and decision making has been characterized by fear. You find yourself clinging to the first thing that you believe could save you from that place, unaware you could be clinging to old demons with new faces. Some of you may see residue of abusive behavior rising in you, lashing out at loved ones, erratic mood swings, violent episodes. Many others may be dealing with sexual addiction or repulsion and these issues may be haunting you; showing their face in every relationship you develop until something is done about it. The very monster you feared could be growing in you if not properly confronted.

Neglect

FOR SOME OF YOU IT may not have been the threat of violence or verbal abuse that pulled you into your shell of shame and disconnect, neglect, while passive has equally damaging effects. Being grossly neglected by either parent sends strong messages of unworthiness to the mind of a growing little girl. There is no uncertainty of how a parent feels towards a child they neglect. The fact that the parent is visible but not engaging can almost be worse than a parent not being there. A conscious decision was made by either your father or mother to choose drugs, money, sex or some other vice over loving you. This excludes parents who were so consumed with school or work to provide a better life for you. You are fully aware of the difference between a parent who chooses to neglect you from one that is forced to spend time away in attempts to provide a good life for you.

Infidelity

CHEATING DOESN'T JUST happen to a spouse, it's betrayal against the whole family. Unfortunately, some of us had front row seats to one of our parents being trampled via infidelity. It can appear like a mistake that can be easily swept under the rug but only spouses of cheating spouses can attest to the devastation left behind by the tornado that an affair brings. If you witnessed your mom or dad attempt to rise from the ashes of such treatment, you probably have distorted views of intimacy and marriage until this day. Although you were not the direct victim of the infidelity it's impossible to detach from its sting. As a little girl it tramples the Cinderella-like fairy tales of love you once held and teaches you the dark side of relationships before you were even ready to experience them. Although you love both your parents, it's difficult to understand. Why would someone who loves someone else hurt them in such a way? Often times subtle or even blatant resentment can boil within your heart, and you will never view the offending parent the same again. On one hand you're broken because you were dealt a hand you didn't deserve, on another you are terrified because you're not immune from it happening to you. You're terrified of giving your heart because of the possibility that you will be cheated on, and you refuse to surrender your heart to be crushed. Or perhaps the disease was contagious, what started as a blatant disregard of your parent from an unfaithful figure in the home spread into a flaw you find it hard to overcome. You can't help but fall into the scandalous living you witnessed as a child. You saw that it was possible to devalue a partner in a relationship and to break the covenant between man and woman and now you are trapped on that rodent's wheel.

Failed Friendships

THERE CAME A TIME IN your life where it became "uncool" to adopt the values and outlooks of your parents. Especially when it came to most of the important things in life. Things like music, movies, and fashion preferences. You began to unwrap yourself from the leg of daddy and mommy and clung to the opinions of other kids your age; many of whom didn't know any better than you. The inescapable truth is, if we are all broken, then paying more attention to your friends than your parents won't fix the issue. You were more likely to be introduced to a new version of brokenness that you've never known.

Peer pressure and the desire to be accepted amongst friends from pre-teen into late teen years may have consumed your entire middle and high school life. But what happens when a friend lies on you, betrays you, replaces you or even moves away? We underestimate the effects of shattered friendships on our maturing minds

Failed Romance

WE CANNOT TALK ABOUT true healing until will take time to deal with the residue left behind by our exes. For many of us, thoughts of our *first loves* have been tainted by the heartbreak that followed. Although your first bad relationships may seem like springboards to your current situation, they may have just been a continuation of a mishandling of your heart by different hands. Let's get one thing clear, this section is not about your ex, darn him. It's about you. If you continue to hold your ex responsible for your betterment, you will be waiting until you're old and gray, and still will end up disappointed. Although you can't prevent all bad seeds from entering the bunch, we can all be very certain, that the *you* today, with all your wisdom and experience would probably not have given your ex the inch to have taken the mile that led to your early ruin. We're sure there were smoking red flags that the healthy and healed *you* would have caught too soon in advance for your heart to be so accessible. However, we can't change the past, and truly, you did let them in, and now you're dealing with the effects of it.

Apart from experiences with your family, your early romantic relationships had the most impact on your outlook on all future relationships. Those first days, weeks, months or years spent with who we now can refer to as your ex have shaped who you see in the mirror today. Your vulnerability, your level of trust, even your preferences.

We don't believe it's fair to your future that your ex has so much say in the way that you will love tomorrow. It takes intention to redeem a heart contaminated by the hands of someone who didn't know how to steward it well. But there is a promise land amidst this wilderness.

Some of you may remember the story of Joseph in the Bible. He was a young man who was given a dream by God that he would be a ruler. But his brothers got jealous of his outlandish imagination and his father's favor on him. They plotted to kill him and ended up selling him into slavery. Joseph eventually went from slavery into prison. When he got to prison it would've seemed convenient to curse God, and to doubt the dreams God gave him for the future. With human eyes his brothers who betrayed him became a roadblock to God's blissful plan for his life. Joseph ended up interpreting a dream for Egypt's Pharaoh while in prison and was released and promoted to a high commanding official in the land. Joseph only realized in the end that if it wasn't for his brothers' wickedness toward him, he wouldn't have been able to walk in the purpose God had ordained for his life. He declared to his brothers after all was said and done in Genesis 50:

"You intended to harm me, but God intended it all for good."

We want you to view your trauma and storm filled relationship with your ex through Joseph's lenses. God allowed you to face what you faced so you could help others. You may relate to Joseph. You endured your trials not simply because you had a hard life but because God wants you to see who you truly are in Him and cause you to move towards fruitful relationships for His glory. We're not saying you will never hurt again, but there's a difference in outcome when the bad guys come for a helpless child and when they come for a skilled assassin. You will be equipped to confront new mountains with new faith and wisdom. By the end of this book, we encourage you to write your exes thank you letters! If it weren't for the garbage you went through with them, you couldn't have discovered the whole you.

Summary

THROUGHOUT THIS CHAPTER we delved into some of the many possible roots of your brokenness. It would be impossible to truly discuss every possible road that led you to issues that may be hindering your growth. Perhaps reading certain parts of this chapter disturbed you, or worse re-triggered feelings of anger, sadness, abandonment and betrayal. It's okay. We encourage you to let it happen. Often times in detoxing processes it's said that things may get worse before they gets better. We believe the same is true about your healing. You've spent years upon years burying the bitter effects of past trauma or even taking self-defeating actions to mask them from slipping through the cracks of your daily life. This book was designed for just that. We desire for you to confront what you've long accepted as normal and shatter it to keep it from shattering you any longer. The emotions and thoughts stirring within you is a very strong sign that you're exactly where you need to be. Facing your issues for what they are and staring them in the eye is the only way you can move forward.

You must understand that all the trauma and brokenness you endured communicated its own truth to you. Mind you, we said "it's truth". All truth outside of what God says about you should be made null and void. And what does God say about you?

Well, if you feel you were not loved he's telling you, "I love you with an everlasting love",

If you feel abandoned he's saying, "I will never leave you nor forsake you." If you feel undeserving he's telling you, "I died for you, I go to prepare a place for you"

If you fear no one cares for you, He says, "Come to me all you of heavy laden, I will give you rest because I care for you."

We want you to actively go back through the parts of this chapter that screamed out at you. We have addressed your early episodes of your upbringing to discover what complex trauma is and how you may have been impacted devastatingly or even subtly in your life. We explored our natural instinct towards emotional chemotherapy, attempting to survive with our wounds instead of seeking for true healing. But we are challenging you to move past your frozen state. Take the initiative and make steps to recover you. Find a mirror and speak aloud. Be courageous enough to say, "Yes, I __(your name here)___ experienced complex trauma as a child. I was hurt by being abandoned by my father, mother (or both). I am still hurt about my parents getting a divorce, I am still bothered that my parent cheated on my other parent. I was devastated by the breakup of my past relationship. I did and still do need loving touches, offerings, presence and verbal unification to experience a whole love for myself and others. I have been affected by tumultuous relationships I've either witnessed or experienced in my past. I admit and accept my past." Whatever applies to you, we invite you to be open and honest enough to admit it to yourself. But then move on to say, "I am not my past. I am not the trauma I endured. It does not have power over me." With such a clear and powerful statement, it is possible to begin affirming all of the amazing and harmonious things that God has to say about you and is doing for you.

Meghan has parents that failed to give her true offerings that would support her passion. How do you think Meghan's trauma will most likely affect her long term?

 A. She'll become an offering machine; giving all that she has to the Lord and everyone around her.

 B. She will struggle with this lacking pillar and may seek it out from others in unhealthy ways.

 C. She'll pray about it and God will resolve it for her immediately.

Your Reasoning:

Brittany had parents who were consumed with their careers and didn't give Brittany any quality presence. How do you think Brittany's trauma will most likely impact her character moving forward?

A. Brittany might become mean and anti-social to everyone who doesn't want to hang out with her.
B. Brittany will seek to drown her loneliness in alcoholism.
C. Brittany will probably take it personally and believe that forming connections is difficult and will more readily accept relationships that don't serve her or build her up in any significant way.

Your Reasoning:

Rhonda didn't receive enough loving touches from her family growing up. Why do you think her problematic childhood didn't evolve into more positive behavior by adulthood?

    A. Because loving touch was her greatest need, she was unable to cope with such a profound void of it. And so, it became exceedingly difficult not to seek physical interaction in whatever form she could find.
    B. Rhonda wanted to feel like people would listen to her. But now she can't trust anyone except God.
    C. Rhonda wanted to feel like a kid again.

Your Reasoning:

Dana's parents didn't shower her with verbal unification. In what ways can this broken pillar impact her psychologically over the long term?

    A. Dana might struggle to say nice things to people out of jealousy.

    B. Dana will be just fine.

    C. Dana could develop a defensive nature and find it difficult to both admit her needs and to give others what she is missing.

Your Reasoning:

Chapter 3: The Faces of Brokenness

Toxic Relationships

W e've used the word broken quite a bit thus far, and for good reason. We really want you to grasp the depth of these issues but mainly because we want you to deprogram from dysfunction. There are situations that you have endured relationally that you have normalized to keep you sane. In this chapter we will take time to see how our past hurts have affected us in our current relationships, and how to be honest with who we've become. While reading this book, it's okay to step out of the armor you've collected and worn up until now. Be encouraged. Know that you know you're not alone. There's no need to read with the filter of a facade; we all are indeed broken in many ways.

Our Families

IN A SPOKEN WORD PIECE floating around on the Internet called *Identity Crisis of Misfit*, a poet says,

"Even nature proves, that the best way to know something is to know what something came from."

That statement may ring truer for some of us than for others. But one thing can't be mistaken. Your family had a major impact on shaping your world view. You may read this and think, "But I am nothing like my family." Our reply to that is, "Well...precisely!" You needed to see and understand how they thought and functioned so that you could embrace some of their ways and repel those that didn't serve you. From there, you were able to carve out a path that was distinct from theirs. And that, is as clear a sign of their choices impacting you as any.

But is it possible that our relationships with our family members—even if not strained, may have painted an incomplete picture of love for us? It's highly likely if you're experiencing any level of brokenness in your family, every member of the family has been and continues to be affected by it as well. The better we can identify the dysfunctional modes of communication, thought processes and functions of our family, the easier it will be to find the hairline cracks within ourselves.

What is your relationship like with your parents today? Were you dying to be set free from the oppression of their household? Have they become distant estranged figures who merely share your DNA and last name? Do you consistently recall past thoughts of your times with them with a lingering resentment? Were you abandoned, belittled, or abused by them? After learning about the roots of your own bitterness, do you feel like your parents failed you? Do believe that they didn't put forth enough effort to understand and love you the way you were programmed to be loved?

If you answered yes to any one of these questions, it's likely that you still have an unhealthy relationship with your parents. It's true you may still attend the barbecues, and perhaps you do stay in contact. But that doesn't negate the fact that there are elements of your relationship that have yet to be reconciled.

What about your siblings? Do you feel like your relationships with them were seasonal? They were the kids you grew up with, but outside of that being around each other takes your joy away. Do you feel your brother(s) or sister(s) owe you for not showing you what it truly means to be blood? Were they unkind to you? Were they indifferent to your existence? Did they not stand up for your when you needed them? Did they choose their other friends over you? If you harbor any of these sentiments towards your sibling, it's likely you have a toxicity severing what should be an unbreakable bond.

Reconciliation is Power

YOU HAVE THE POWER to heal it. Sometimes we are waiting on God while he's waiting on us. However, the steps towards healing a broken family won't start from the weaker links. Forgiveness is not just a nice thing to do, it's the key to your peace. It's such a crucial component to spiritual wholeness in Matthew 5:23-24 scripture tells us,

> *"So if you are offering your gift at the altar and there remember that your brother has something against you, leave your gift there before the altar and go. First be reconciled to your brother, and then come and offer your gift."*

It also says in Mark 11:25:

"And when you stand praying, if you hold anything against anyone, forgive them, so that your Father in heaven may forgive you your sins."

Forgiveness is an essential anchor in our own salvation. Forgiveness is the only way we are able to experience peace with God. A Holy God, initiates forgiveness to us broken sinners.

Friends

AS YOU APPROACHED TEENAGE years, there was a desire stirring within you. That desire was the need to know that someone understood you, cared about you, and had your best interests at heart other than your parents. When you begin to think about all the time spent, all the secrets and girl time you shared with your childhood friend(s), it almost makes the idea of familial relationships seem like an appetizer. A solid friendship was a bit more like the main course. Friendships don't necessarily have to fail to be broken. However, due to the fact that you were unaware of the depths and nuances of your own shortcomings, it would be virtually impossible to have built whole, transparent, and honest friendships without letting our masks get in the way. (We will talk more about these masks later on in the chapter.)

Answer this, if your friends were to take a polygraph test and were asked about what type of friend you were, what would they say? Would they describe you as selfish, closed off, insensitive, a gossiper, or unforgiving? Or a better question might be, are you the friend that you would want to have? Think about the small disagreements you've had with those you've called friends, is there a pattern with the topics of contention? Are you accused of the same things time and time again. Is everyone else 'trippin', or is it possible that you are a major contributor to the problems you face in your friendships today. Being a good friend isn't solely thinking about your strengths but rather reflecting on your willingness to improve upon your weaknesses.

Whether you know it or not, your toxic behaviors have dragged you into friendships that may not be completely healthy. The fact that you've maintained certain friendships may not be based on your great character but their high tolerance for your destructive traits.

Ourselves

THE MOST APPARENT FACE of brokenness exists in the relationship we have with ourselves, which is the most important relationship we can have. Referring back to the idea of emotional chemotherapy, we suffer dire consequences when we use our frailty to attempt to fix the soul God breathed into us.

Addictions

OFTEN TIMES WE DON'T know that we are addicted until it's too late. But we can assure you that our addictions are usually signs that we're trying to fix something that is out of order. Think about food addictions, what may start as a little over consumption of our favorite comfort food can quickly spiral out of control into a dangerous obsession that we can't seem to control. But there is think one word in the phrase "comfort food" that illuminates the essence of the problem. We try to comfort or coddle our painful gashes instead of allowing surgery to take place. The overuse of neutral things like food, social media, and even television have become square blocks, forced into the round holes of our hearts. The fact that we keep going back to something that doesn't satisfy, proves that the well we keep running to drink from was never designed to quench our thirst. Even though the objects of some of our obsessions may not be harmful in and of themselves, our mishandling of them prove that our firewalls of discipline have been conquered by our desire to comfort our wounds in our own strength. Maybe it isn't food for you, it could be drugs, alcohol, sex, or anything you allowed to have power over you. Think to yourself, are there any behaviors you engage in that you enjoy in the moment but brings shame and emptiness to you in the end? Any actions you engage in, when behind closed doors that you would be embarrassed to disclose? Do you ever feel like you can't help it? Chances are you may be addicted; addicted to trying to escape from something you should be confronting and healing from. It's time to look that monster square in the eyes and fight for your whole you. You can't be content while in shambles.

Denial

OVER AND OVER AGAIN you've heard us say it's time to confront. We will continue to press this button because confession and admission are the paved road towards true redemption. When we deny we are lying to ourselves thinking we are protecting ourselves. But from what? Can you imagine a gunshot victim stumbling into an emergency room with a critical wound to her torso? Nurses surround her and ask her what's going on. Instead of her showing them the injury she, with agony smeared across her face, uses her hands to cover the bloody opening saying, "I'm good, I'm okay." This victim will receive eyes of sympathy, but no hands of intervention. It's only a matter of time until she bleeds out and forfeits her life. This victim is you, if you're actively revealing symptoms of problems that are apparent to others but refusing to own up to them. Pride is telling you that admitting your issues will damage the way people view you. Have you considered that your damaged view of yourself is more problematic? Are you more interested in living a lie and accepting the facade of being okay? Or do you sincerely want to be healed? Denial is the enemy of healing. When you become more interested in being well than making it seem like you're well, you will experience a revolution.

How Broken People Love

Fearful Lover

SYMPTOMS OF A FEARFUL lover include but are not limited to these traits: insecurity, escapism, control, jealousy, abusiveness, cold-heartedness and stubbornness.

It's impossible to truly access your capacity to love or be loved when consumed with fear. This is why fear is such an enemy to loving and fruitful relationships, it keeps people from taking the steps necessary towards vulnerability and trust. Are you a fearful lover? Let's take a look at what that is and how you got here. It would seem that a fearful lover would be limited to those who are reserved or timid in relationships. While this may be true in some cases, fearful lovers are actually skilled at concealing their anxiety and wearing other traits as masks which are often harmful to others. As a fearful lover you are prone to running from modes that you aren't emotionally able to handle. As Kiyanna shared, my (Ezekiel) fear of rejection plagued me since childhood. I was insecure in many ways, so I longed to be fully accepted by everyone I valued. When we first got married, the adrenaline of love blinded us to some of my issues. I didn't know loving touch was a pillar that communicated love for me and it wasn't the main pillar that communicated love for my wife so we ran into problems. Our deepest cracks would be most evident after an argument. Once our disagreement was in the air, I would wait a few minutes then creep up behind to hug her from the back and she would escape from my grasp like I had leprosy. I had no idea that her heart would be settled with honest, gentle words and my loving presence alone. I could only view the situation from my limited view. If I was sour after an argument it would cheer me all the way up to be hugged and kissed. I would spiral in to bouts of silent anger from the rejection I thought I was experiencing and ran to my secret vice, pornography. I was too prideful to tell her it hurt my feelings when she would respond in certain ways, so I didn't give a chance for mutual clarity. My fearful love tendencies caused me to control my emotional vulnerability by creating a false world of intimacy through porn. It didn't last and it made me feel disgusting. After confession, much counseling and proper understanding of each other and our respective past wounds, we grew and flourished in love. As a fearful lover, you make a habit of running. Running manifests in many ways, from avoiding conversations, situations, or hiding from seasons of a relationship that demand access to your heart. You tend to bottle up your true feelings. The idea of laying your true feelings on the table strips the bullet proof vest from your chest and—boom—you're vulnerable enough to be hurt again. You may find a safe haven in escapism, you look for a way out of any situation that pushes you into a place that perpetuates your worst fears of being rejected or abandoned. You can also run by fighting. You can become hostile, controlling, or even violent when you perceive that you're mentally placed in a situation that reminds you of trauma that has scarred you. You believe that if you can control the actions of others and the way you are perceived, you won't be hurt. This dynamic is also known as having trust issues. Due to past wounds we refuse to allow people to enter our sphere of our most vulnerable selves. But how can you truly love and be loved while keeping your loved one at the fringes of the relationship? The walls you've built to keep others from being able to hurt have begun to isolate you from those who may be approaching with good intentions. Staying in this place will keep you frozen and you will never gain the emotional capacity to sustain a long-term relationship. The most difficult task for a fearful lover, is confrontation. It may scare you to death to be left in states of vulnerability and helplessness. But the honest truth is, if you refuse to overcome your fears, they will eventually overcome you.

Dana's calls are going straight to Martin's voicemail now. He's on a business trip in Miami and her mind is running nonstop. Dana has seen Martin's cute coworkers but she's more afraid of vacationing perfect bodied women running around everywhere ready to snatch her man in the blink of an eye. She tried to find a ticket so she could be by his side and give dirty looks to every girl that comes even remotely his way. Her friends tell her to ease up, Martin has never given her a reason to worry before and her jealous ways are beginning to become overwhelming for everyone.

Dana has no clue that she's overly controlling and jealous. But the deeper issues surrounding these destructive traits are tied to her deepest fears. Her control and jealousy are all weak attempts to hide the fact that she's afraid of being alone and terrified of getting her heart broken again. You're not controlling because you want to be a bad person. You don't exude anger because it's fun. You've allowed your flawed coping mechanism to turn you into someone that's difficult to appreciate in the mirror. You control in an attempt to bend people and circumstances in ways that are less threatening to your most tender self. You keep piling on the armor for wars you keep creating. You must understand that the world doesn't work that way, and neither does love. Your willingness to be vulnerable when it counts and letting God work is not a sign of weakness but strength.

Anger issues are a symptom of fear. While anger is a natural human response to injustice or failure there's a distinct difference between healthy and unhealthy anger. When you allow your anger to overtake your logic, you lose self-control and become a danger to others and yourself. An angry person is an unreasonable person. Think about it. How many times have you had to take back something you said in anger? How many people have been hurt and even killed after someone let their anger overcome them? The beast of anger can either be dealt with by reacting to it or taking action against it. The way you take action against anger is through open and honest communication. If anger plagues you, then take the initiative towards your own healing. Turn to someone you can trust—who is willing to listen——and be honest with both them and yourself about how you feel. Someone who is spiritually mature enough to speak sense and life into you so that you can see things with a Godly perspective. James 5 says:

"Confess your faults one to another, and pray one for another, that ye may be healed."

But not only your faults but your wounds, and your fears, there is truly healing power in communication.

In many cases, the lack of a father in the home handicaps your ability to love fearlessly. The security and reassurance a father's presence gave you was undeniable. When you looked at your father, you were able to see the mature, experienced, and wise leader of your home. His words of affirmation and correction molded you and strengthened your demeanor. When daddy was home it was clear that authority was in place, no problem was too big for him to fix, and the home had a sturdy backbone. Imagine being on an airplane, 30,000 feet in the air. You're comfortably seated and relaxed until you begin to feel bumping, and violent shaking. You've heard about this before, it's turbulence. You eagerly await the pilot's explanation of what's happening. And sure enough, the calm and collected voice blankets the passengers from the intercom. He lets them know that they are experiencing a bit of turbulence at the moment.

Everything is fine and it'll be over shortly. Something inside of you feels ease again. You believe that pilot knows what he's doing, where he's going and because he's there, you're safe. Now imagine the same instance but instead of the voice of the pilot, you see a flight attendant running frantically from the cockpit yelling, "the pilot is gone!" You immediately go into panic mode. You're faced with two options, give up and let the plane crash and die or run to the cockpit, and attempt to fly the plane in a panicked state yourself, crash then die. Neither of those options are that appealing right? That's exactly what happens when a father is not present in his daughter's life. While some crawl in a corner to perish, some of us run to the cockpit, terrified, and attempt to pilot our lives in our father's place. We weren't trained for it. And the result is often crashing and burning in the relationships with our significant others.

If you were unable to properly grow from girlhood to womanhood because of the lack of a solid male figure in your home, you have likely developed tactics to deal with the scared girl inside of you. The little girl that doesn't have all the answers, the girl that is trying to find her way; deaf and blindfolded. A girl that has to either repel the sight of a man or give boys an opportunity to try out the pilot's seat in her heart.

She is still suspended in the air, not knowing what to do next and it reminds her of the lost little girl who was abandoned so many years ago. A panicking passenger on a plane going down without a pilot. No matter what it takes, she would do anything to keep herself from feeling the reality of this.

Insecure Lover

SYMPTOMS OF THIS TYPE of lover include but are not limited to these traits: Low self-esteem, compliance with mistreatment, jealousy, and people pleasing.

"You mean the world to me. When we kiss it's magic, I can't wait to see you again." The dimly lit screen, stained with that catastrophic text that still plagues Brittany two weeks after she saw it.

She met Rodney in college. They hit it off and quickly became more than friends. Rodney is exciting, smart and handsome, so Brittany couldn't help but show him off every chance she got. Brittany has been imagining what life would be like married to Rodney and what type of father he would be.

When she read that daunting text from who he had saved as Daniel, Brittany's world came crashing down. She knew Rodney had a falling out with Daniel years ago because of his temper.

but she always gave him the benefit of the doubt. Brittany's friends saw the signs from the beginning but she refused to take them seriously. She believes it's her only chance to be with a man with such great qualities. She isn't willing to give it up so easily. "Nobody's perfect," is usually how she responds. Brittany finally reaches out to this mystery person. The person continues to say hello, the voice is familiar. Brittany asks "Rhonda is that you?! The stranger quickly hangs up. Brittany looks at the contact details and drops the phone as if her hand went limp. She collapses to the floor in a lake of tears and disappointment.

She's broken because she knows she and Rodney have nothing. But something deep down inside doesn't want to let go of the dream of marrying him. She chooses to stay quiet and let this violent storm pass because she can't fathom there's someone out there that would want her.

Are you an insecure lover? The word secure means exactly what it sounds like. Security is tied to things like safety, but even more than safety, confidence in your safety. When someone is insecure they aren't confident they are safe. Safe from what? Safe from being unloved, safe from being undesired, safe from being worthless. But how could a person ever have arrived here?

In chapter 2 we talked a lot about the pillars of Whole Love necessary for healthy emotional development. Deficiency of any of the pillars discussed that could have bred insecurity within you—specifically the Pillars off verbal unification and loving touch. As a child it was vital that you weren't simply raised but loved in ways that made you certain you're loved. That's exactly what Insecure lovers do not have; certainty. When if you are an insecure lover, you're uncertain if you are truly valued, you tend to operate pessimistically. You're likely to expect rejection, to be unappreciated, or undesired. You could have also easily been made to feel insecure by abuse, or a toxic relationship early in life that communicated you weren't worth it.

It would be one thing if insecurity was a toxic trait that only affected you. However, it affects you, and everyone you love, and those you've yet to love. Insecurity keeps you from expecting good. It keeps you from owning the value you offer in spaces that you occupy. It makes you more hesitant to take risks that lead to advancement because you don't believe you're able to bet on yourself. There's always someone more capable, smarter, or better looking than you. This mindset opens the door for low standards, willingness to accept mistreatment and an unwillingness to walkway from toxic relationships. If this mindset persists, you could be building your future on an undesired foundation.

Insecurity can also show up in your inability to find value in all you are. You have never been fully appreciated for your value in certain areas so the moment you are celebrated in one area you retreat to the refuge of that moment, and build your self-esteem around that. This is why it's easy to find people who seem to be extremely showy about certain aspects of their lives. With the new age of social media, it's even more of an epidemic. Pay close attention to those who are obsessed with posting their bodies, or certain features on their social media page, allowing comments and likes to feed their egos. Truth be told, not all of the Individuals who post like this are full of themselves. Some are highly insecure. They crawl behind their most celebrated feature or asset because they are uncertain about their true value in other areas. They run to the applause, searching to be affirmed. It's very common to become so addicted to the acknowledgement and affirmation of others that the pressure to be made sure of your value in relationships cannot be never be satisfied. This is why basing your security on the fleeting opinions of other people is a bad idea. God has already made us certain that we are not worthless. In John 15:13 it reads

"Greater love has no one than this: to lay down one's life for one's friends."

Nothing tells us—or rather reminds us—that we are valuable more than the truth that Christ laid down his life for us. This truth we must use to combat insecurity. After all insecurity is in essence being doubtful of God's action of love towards us. It's rooted in the question the serpent asked Eve in the garden, "Did God really say..?" How can we truly be insecure about our value while believing the Creator of this world died specifically for us?

Selfish Lover

SYMPTOMS OF THIS TYPE of lover include but are not limited to unfaithfulness, entitlement, lack of commitment, lack of discipline, lack of moral values, and victimization.

Rhonda walks towards the counter to pick up her latte. She locks eyes with him, the new employee with dark brown eyes, caramel complexion and muscular body. He hands her a straw and she notices a wedding ring on his left hand. Rhonda smiles at him, and strikes up a conversation. She asks if he has a social media account. He tells her he has an account but doesn't use it often, because he's busy being a husband and father. Rhonda is turned on by his willingness to have integrity, because it's a challenge. She asks for the profile name, he tells her. Rhonda says thank you and makes she walks away with a hip sway he won't forget. She swiftly sends a direct message to his inbox telling him she can be his personal barista. Inwardly, she believes she can get him to crack with just a little more time and effort. Her phone vibrates and lights up against the table, she checks the screen and sees "Brittany" calling again. She quickly declines the call because she has her eyes set on a new exciting adventure, a married man.

Rhonda has no idea that she is a whirlwind of destruction operating as a selfish lover because she lacked focused love from her father growing up. The phrase selfish lover is honestly an oxymoron however we will continue to use this phrase for the sake of consistency. As we saw in chapter 2, true love at its core requires you to give of yourself sacrificially. It's very likely that if you are a selfish lover you may not be aware because it's difficult to be significantly introspective when most of your time is devoted to fulfilling your needs.

It's quite easy to view this type of lover as the evil one, the one who needs the least understanding because the unacceptable traits associated with it. But before we point fingers, let's figure out how it happens and what it can possibly look like in your life.

Selfishness in its rawest human form is a natural quality of mankind. By nature, we are always seeking for means to keep ourselves alive by eating, avoiding danger, and even grooming to keep ourselves clean. Loving ourselves is not only natural but it's Godly. God expects us as humans to love ourselves as seen in Matthew 22:37:

"...love your neighbor as you love yourself."

If Christ expected us to have a weak and dismissive love for ourselves, he would never recommend we offer it to our neighbors. However, when you value yourself without considering the needs of others it becomes problematic. But how and when does this shift happen? How do we go from natural self-love to destructive selfishness? It can happen a number of ways.

Sometimes parents can love you into selfishness and entitlement. When your parents fail to communicate the weight of reward and consequence, you are never able to recognize the rule of reaping and sowing. You begin to feel you are deserving of what you never earned and can get away with anything.

However, a lack of focused love also could have led you to selfish ways. When parents are inconsistent with their outpouring of attention, affection and presence with you. It's almost like finding those two-dollar bills growing up. We never in a rush to spend them because we never knew when we would come across them again. Your needs not being fulfilled in some way as a child was so distasteful emotionally, having it became an idol, the little god that your emotions held on to. So even if a parent gave you some attention, loving gifts, and their presence, you viewed it as a rare commodity and began to inwardly create habits that would promote the preservation of this commodity over others. You began to feel that if you didn't take advantage of what you believed belonged to you, you would lose it, and it would hurt, and now your behavior would reflect this.

Rhonda knows that what she's doing is wrong, but because she's a selfish lover, even things that are wrong or inconvenient are not enough to hinder her.

Selfishness by default makes you inconsiderate. How can you consider another's feelings, when you're too wrapped up with what you want at the moment? An unfaithful person in a relationship doesn't mean they don't have genuine feelings for a person, or that they are evil at the core. The problem is selfishness has become a faulty lens over your eyes. Those lenses cloud every meaningful and valuable thing in your life outside of your immediate wants. While you actually do believe in God, like your job, have feelings for a boyfriend and know that it would destroy you to be cheated on, you can't see these things as clear and as vividly as your wants. So, you're willing to risk everything at the expense of what is most clear. Selfishness has distorted your value system to the point that everything else will always fall second.

If you're unfaithful you may also have other toxic traits in your life like a lack of self-discipline and commitment, especially in relationships. You may be dealing with entitlement. You are willing to manipulate others to get what you feel you rightfully deserve. In a healthy relationship, the heart beat and fuel to keep it thriving is the idea of two people growing and learning and striving to be better for each other. You're willing to say no to advances from others, shut down flirtation, and once you're in a relationship, put in the work to stay in it and grow in it. Your commitment level is high because you're able to see the value in how someone else contributes to your life. If you're selfish, your mind is always bent on what you're not getting and what could possibly be better out there, so staying with one person exclusively long term seems like a daunting task.

Be honest with yourself. Are you a selfish lover? Now that you can imagine how you got here it's possible to be better. You must remove the lenses that have kept you from seeing the significance of the valuable things in life. Christ teaches,

"If anyone would come after me, let him deny himself and take up his cross and follow me. For whoever would save his life will lose it, but whoever loses his life for my sake will find it."

Matthew 16:25

The practice of self-denial is a practice that actively combats selfishness. It says that there are things more important than my worldly, immediate desires, like honoring God and showing love to others. You cannot continue to allow your wants to keep you from living a life that honors God because at the end of the day, you can never truly be satisfied without Him. When you're done trampling your morals and the hearts of those who potentially love you, you still won't feel complete. This is because you're God-conscious. Living and loving like God is the most fulfilling way of life. Trying to avoid this route will only lead you towards a life of emptiness and isolation.

Desperate Lover

SYMPTOMS OF THIS TYPE of lover include but are not limited to: people pleasing, self-sabotage, low integrity, dishonest lifestyle.

Meghan sits in her car alone, in the parking lot of a burger stand near Sunset Blvd in Hollywood, CA. She ponders on how the last two years of her life have brought her to this moment as she twists her wedding around her finger. She just tied the knot with Daniel two weeks ago and just moved to Los Angeles from Detroit so that Daniel could pursue acting and be closer to the beach. She should be happier, right? Except for the fact that she had a passion for teaching young girls the art of dance in the inner city of Detroit. She was already in the early stages of launching her after school program. She's shared her heart for the inner city with Daniel but he seems to brush it off and tells her she needs to dream bigger and she won't have to worry about anything when he makes it big.

Meghan gets angry and scrambles to her phone to erase the social media profile Daniel convinces her to create. Her profile picture is a crisp headshot and her status describes her interests as reality tv acting and high-profile social clubs. As soon as she is about to click the delete button, Daniel calls and says "you're never going to believe this, I got us both roles on a new internet reality drama. We're going to be famous!" Meghan seemingly lights up, thinking to herself, "As long as he's happy, I'm good. I guess I can get used to living this dream. Even if it isn't mine."

If you're a desperate lover you have likely had a longing for love and affection from before you could remember. You are probably more familiar with abandonment and neglect than the next person. This void you experienced made you a desperate lover, willing to cling to anyone to fill the void; even if it's at your own detriment. Though an optimist you are more likely to give up on your own goals and dreams to make others happy. In fact, making others happy could be one of your biggest flaws. We discussed how self-denial is such a positive trait but a desperate lover has no boundaries when it comes to taking themselves out of the equation. You are willing to go to great lengths to show the person that you love that you're down for them. But you pay little attention to your mental and emotional health.

As a desperate lover you are more likely to conform your values to whoever you want to love you back. In an effort to please them you can find yourself being dishonest about who you are and what you believe. Your fear of abandonment drives you to please at all costs, and you always eventually become the casualty of choice.

God did not design you to live a life of self-sabotage. You can never reach your full potential if you're always willing to sacrifice yourself and future to please others. Your desperation to get and/or keep a relationship can be harmful if there is not mutual love, effort, and understanding.

Summary

THERE ARE MANY FACES of brokenness. Some may have stemmed from the various roots of abandonment, betrayal and lack of love and they have seeped into the way we relate to and love others in our lives at this moment. First, we unmasked toxic relationships, from our families, to our friends, and even ourselves. We then discussed how our broken pasts shaped the way we love today. We looked at what it means to be fearful, selfish, insecure, and desperate as a lover. Some of you may identify with more than one type of lover. Others may only identify with fragments of one. There are some of you that have vividly been in relationships with people who ooze many of the toxic traits we went through in this chapter. No matter how you connect with these areas of brokenness, the truth of it all is that you connect. We all do.

This is why we continue to harp on the fact that you're not alone, but if we break together let's now make a commitment to heal together. And once we embark upon this journey of wholeness, it's our duty to bring others along for the ride, isn't that what God's purpose looks like? Now let's move towards healing and how that plays out tangibly. Our sister, you are on your way, "...Rise and go. Your faith makes you whole."

Dana is a fearful lover; jealous and controlling; overcome by the powerlessness caused by her father's absence. What type of toxic lover do you think she is most likely to attract?

A. A fearful lover

B. An insecure lover
C. A selfish lover
D. A desperate lover

Your Reasoning:

Brittany is an insecure lover plagued by thoughts of unworthiness. What type of toxic lover do you think she is most likely to attract?

A. A fearful lover
B. An insecure lover
C. A selfish lover
D. A desperate lover

Your Reasoning:

Meghan is a desperate lover. She feels she's stuck in a marriage where her passions are being ignored, but holds on because she feels having someone is better than having no one at all. What type of toxic lover do you think she is most likely to attract?

A. A fearful lover
B. An insecure lover
C. A selfish lover
D. A desperate lover

Your Reasoning:

Rhonda is a selfish lover. Promiscuous with integrity as strong as withering thread. What type of toxic lover do you think she is most likely to attract?

    A. A fearful lover
    B. An insecure lover
    C. A selfish lover
    D. A desperate lover

Your Reasoning:

Chapter 4: The Power of Internal Healing

<img width=50>

You now understand the factors from your past experiences that have contributed to the person you are and how they can be a hindrance to your journey. This knowledge is vital as understanding and coming to terms with your past is the only way you can move forward on your path to wholeness. Every experience in life plays a part in shaping who you are. But *you* are ultimately responsible for how it shapes you. We must understand how we can use our experiences to positively shape ourselves and our environment.

Living as a more whole person requires we live a more deliberate life. We must have a constant awareness of how we perceive our world and how it affects our psyche. This doesn't mean that we should have to expend a ton of effort keeping every part of our lives under a microscope as we experience it. But we should be mindful and pay attention to our reactions to people and situations, as well as what causes our reactions. That way we can spend a portion of time reflecting on whether or not we feel those reactions are in line with who we want to be and, more importantly, who God wants us to be.

In this chapter, we will discuss the concept of consumption (or what we put into ourselves). Our minds and bodies are in a constant state of consumption. Everything we take in subtly alters us. We have little control over how the things we consume affect our body. However, we can control how our mind processes certain stimuli by viewing the world through new lenses; lenses that we wear to perceive in the way that we know an upright Christian should. This ultimately, alters the effect these stimuli have on us; allowing us to better manage stress and hardship. To achieve this, we must have an understanding of four processes:

- How we view ourselves
- How we view our environment
- How we think
- How we are sustained

Before we delve into these, we must first understand why achieving wholeness matters and equip ourselves mentally and spiritually for this journey.

Embracing the Beauty of Process

WE HEAR THE PHRASE, "God is working on me" all the time. It's often a cliché used to defend bad character. But indeed, we are a work in progress. As we mentioned in the first chapter, wholeness is a journey; not a specific destination. In this microwave generation, we tend to become agitated with the natural process of blossoming. If you've ever been on a real weight loss and fitness journey you can appreciate the value of process. We know we want to lose weight and see definition but we can't simply snap our fingers and see the change. We have to endure grueling cardio, resistance training, and—worst of all—change our diets to actually achieve significant progress. One thing we've learned that continues to remain true is that going hard is good, but going again is essential. Consistency and time will always outdo short lived bursts. The sweat, the pain, and the choice to eat salad over ice cream is something we have to endure in order to achieve our dream physique or state of health. And embracing the beautiful pain of process deters us from falling into toxic habits that will take us in a different direction altogether.

As we face our failures, and experiences we must do so with new lenses. We have to begin to view ourselves and the world around us the way God does. This is where simply knowing the Word of God is not enough. We must apply it to our lives to see true change. Whether we realize it or not, we process our lives with a fault first filter. Think about it. You take 75 selfies then scroll through them with 'Inspector Gadget' eyes to weed out the blemished images, all in an effort to find the perfect one to share. We believe that the selfie which exhibits the least flaws, is the most valuable one. It's unfortunate this method translates to our realities where we attempt to tuck the imperfect versions of ourselves into the delete folder, and believe that only the one that mirrors perfection is worthy of consumption. But there's one problem with this method; no matter which version of you is inconvenient or uncomfortable, at the end of the day it's still you. It's true sometimes your smile is crooked, or maybe you blinked a bit too long, but darling, it's still you. The real you that doesn't seem quite shareable is still the you that God loves. In fact, God's character throughout scripture highlights his willingness to choose the weak and undesirable. In 1st Samuel, God goes to the house of Jesse to choose the next King of Israel. After Jesse presented all his mighty agile sons for selection, he ended up choosing the least likely candidate, the one who physically was unfit to lead his sheep much less a Kingdom. God sees beyond what the world sees and he is not turned off by our shortcomings.

We Were Worth Dying For

IT'S APPARENT THAT God values us as his children. To begin to walk with new lenses we have to begin to embrace this value despite our pasts. But even more so we need to view our failures through our newfound understanding of our worth. We did nothing to give ourselves innate worth, so no matter what we have done that we aren't proud of we can't take away our worth. Our roots of brokenness, and not being loved well were not barometers of what we deserved. It's time to view things properly. Any way we were failed by others in our past is not an indictment on our value but a failure of another flawed human. We can't live our lives under a cloud of low self-esteem and doubt because of someone else's brokenness.

God forgave you first. The Bible tells us "while we were yet sinners Christ died for us". He imitated forgiveness for our sins by taking it upon himself. How dare we allow shame and guilt to drag us through the mud of life? But truly consider this: a holy, perfect God, who is the only one who can justifiably cast the first stone, is saying, you are free. We literally do not have the right to walk in guilt because we aren't holy enough, nor authorized enough to condemn ourselves. Romans 8:1 reminds us:

> *"Therefore, there is now no condemnation for those who are in Christ Jesus"*

We must believe that if Christ is not condemning us, neither should we.

Often times we feel many of our past deeds are unforgivable, too gruesome for grace. But we must be careful with this ideology. What we are saying is, what Christ did on the cross is not enough to justify me or that we are God himself, rightly judging ourselves in perfect righteousness,

Free yourself from the weight of your past by drowning in the grace God offers his children, it's freeing when you believe it.

3 Ways to Seal Your New Identity

Recognize Who God is

IT'S SIMPLY NOT ENOUGH to have heard of God. Nor is it enough to know that he is good and powerful. It's about knowing who God is to you in and throughout your life. It's pivotal to know what God says about us because who would be better to understand the vessel better than the potter who molded it. God knows how he designed us and why he designed us that way. He's aware of our complexities, and our quirks, he's cognizant of our past and is the writer of our futures.

This here is a no brainer, we just get to know the maker so that we could view the world, pain and love through proper lenses.

The word of God is the most important source for our understanding of who God is. We can read historically who God has been throughout history. We can learn his character through passages painted for us in scripture. We want to learn to value what he values and dismiss what he counts as dung. Only then will we begin to move deeper than a surface experience in humanity towards a rich depth only revealed with spiritual insight.

Make a habit of reading God's word. Find versions of the Bible that are easy for you to understand, connect with people that understand the word and also others eager to learn. Saturate your time with sermons and content that peel back the layers that once made God, vague and distant to one that is personal; one who is acquainted with us. Learning God properly is a prerequisite for seeing *you* properly.

Recognize Who God Says You Are

GOD IS NOT SILENT ABOUT humanity. In fact, the loudest statement he made on our behalf left him lifeless on a rugged cross. God appears to place great value on his fellowship with man. He enjoys man and desires for man to enjoy Him. He gives Life and Life more abundantly! The privilege of life is not to be taken lightly. Begin to view life as an opportunity to deepen your understanding of what God is saying to and about you. Truthfully this is the way we can discover the core of our purpose. We can begin to take note of the beauty of our gifts, quirks and complexities and learn to become vessels that unapologetically shine for God's glory. Our worthiness is not a reflection of our perfection but God's, so we wear His with confidence. Because we bear the image of God and are bestowed with His love, we have to process our value through the sacrifice that was made for us. This stance in Ro-

mans 8 makes war against every contradictory relationship we find ourselves in:

> *"No, in all these things we are more than conquerors through*
> *him who loved us. For I am sure that neither death nor life,*
> *nor angels nor rulers, nor things present nor things to come, nor*
> *powers, nor height nor depth, nor anything else in all creation,*
> *will be able to separate us from the love of God in Christ Jesus*
> *our Lord."*

Romans 8:37-39

Spiritual Freedom Through Prayer

> *But he turned and said to Peter, "Get behind me, Satan! You*
> *are a hindrance to me. For you are not setting your mind on the*
> *things of God, but on the things of man."*

Matthew 16:23

WE DO NOT BELIEVE THE enemy can possess a true disciple of Jesus; whom the Holy Spirit indwells. However, this passage of scripture
we see Christ saying 'get thee behind me Satan' right after Peter makes
a suggestion that he should not die on the cross. How can this be? Can
Satan be this involved when we are believers? The answer is absolutely.
Although the devil cannot possess those of us that are filled with the
Spirit, he can continue to oppress us. He can externally work to hinder
the work of God in our lives. Notice, Jesus spoke directly to the enemy not the person of Peter. This discernment is extremely important.
We have to learn to identify the voice of the enemy and recognize his
strategy. The devil can't force anyone to do anything. All he's done from
the beginning of time is provide alternate suggestions. If God says one
thing, the devil responds with "Did God *really* say?" or "Are you certain
this is what God meant?" God made it clear what His son would en-

dure, and Satan responded by doing all he could to talk Jesus out of his purpose. At first glance the voice of the enemy gives logic, sometimes pleasure or convenience. But the simple fact the voice is an alternative opinion than God's makes it one to flee from.

Once we discover the voice of Satan, we must put him in his rightful place, behind us! We value the word of God so much that it is the only Word we can place in front of us.

"Thy word is a lamp unto my feet, and a light unto my path."

Psalm 119:105.

Without God's word we are lost, the alternative route of the enemy is a glitch in the GPS that will lead us off a cliff into destruction.

In some cases, prayer and fasting is needed. The disciples had a hard time casting out a demon and Jesus told them that this type cannot be dealt with without fasting and prayer. You may be dealing with toxic behaviors, anger, addiction and out workings of demonic activity. The enemy is desperate to frustrate the plan of God in your life. Yield yourself to fasting and prayer and do not be afraid to have your church community rally around you in committed prayer so that you can be free from such attacks. There is true power in prayer. It should not be a last resort, but the first response!

We use the word deliverance because it infers there is a 'coming from' and a 'going to'. God wants you to leave from the state of shame and brokenness to a life of peace and wholeness. Are you experiencing demonic attacks and influence? Do not be afraid to consult your pastor to do what the old-time saints used to say. P.U.S.H. (Pray Until Something Happens).

Mental Freedom through Counseling

Deliverance should not be limited to spiritual activities.

Professional Counseling

WE WHOLEHEARTEDLY BELIEVE in the effectiveness of counseling. In our communities counseling tends to be equated to detention for adults; the place you go to as a punishment for being bad. This couldn't be further from the truth. Counseling is more about stewardship than punishment.

You were given a body and mind to care for. The same way you go to the doctor to check on your physical health, it's vital to take active steps to maintain excellent mental health.

In fact, we believe it should be a proactive step all people should take before even considering marriage. You care too much about who God will call you to marry, to parent, to be a sibling or even a friend to let them have the uncared-for version of you. The version of you that you still don't understand because you haven't had an outside objective opinion, to help you discover parts of you that are harmful to yourself and others. But you can also be given the tools to navigate life with your new understanding in order to better prepare those who you plan to relate with.

How We View Ourselves

WE DON'T HEAR THIS from each other enough but you matter and your life has meaning. God created you with a specific purpose in mind and He wants you to realize and fulfill that purpose. Your ability to fulfill your purpose and become your whole self begins with recognizing your value as a person. Often we experience hardships, failures or traumas in life that bring our worth into question. Perhaps it was a cheating boyfriend. Maybe it was an uncaring or absent parent. It could have even been a harsh boss. Regardless of the source, we've all had experiences that have lowered our self-esteem and made us wonder if we were worthy of the joy we seek. But this does not have to be the case. Simply acknowledging that you have value as a human being is the start of seeing your value as a person; the value God sees in you. Once you know your true value, you'll stop giving people discounts.

All too often we allow the world to determine our value. We compare ourselves to friends, family, coworkers, and even celebrities, using their attributes and accomplishments as baselines to judge ourselves. This is especially true when measuring beauty. What we fail to understand is that there is no objective definition of beauty. Society feeds us cookie cutter examples of beauty based on factors that are easy to commercialize. We see celebrities on TV with "beat" faces so we go out and stock up on makeup. We scroll past models with snatched waists so we order a waist trainer. In extreme cases, we see women with big breasts or booties so we spend thousands on breast or butt implant surgeries or injections. These points are not to judge, but ultimately, the only people who are guaranteed to benefit from this are the people selling the products or performing the surgeries.

The really sad part about all of this is that the benefits we get from these measures are temporary at best if we don't first recognize that we are beautiful with or without the enhancements. It sounds cliché, but beauty really is more than skin deep. Beauty is wholeness. It is a unity of your body, mind, heart, and spirit. Your outward appearance is just one facet of your complete and beautiful self. We are not discounting its importance as it's usually the first aspect of you that people experience. However, women tend to focus too heavily on enhancing beauty at the expense of other aspects. It's easy to blame society and pop culture for this as they play a huge part, but we must also take responsibility for how we let these messages affect us. Ultimately, if you plan on living a fulfilling life with the person God intended you to be with, you must tend to your mind, heart, and spirit in addition to your body.

This begins with understanding who you currently are and accepting that person. Learning to love yourself and understand that you are worthy of love is the foundation of the healthy you. We tend to focus on what we lack or what we need to improve about ourselves. However, we fail to see all our wonderful traits. This warps our self-image and makes it difficult for us to see all that we have to offer. As you take the time to better understand yourself, identify those traits that you love about yourself and celebrate them. This will not only allow you to develop an appreciation for yourself and your positive traits, but it will energize you to work toward improving those things you feel need work.

As you walk this path of self-discovery, you are likely to encounter past traumas. Some of these were due to forces outside of your control. Others may have been a direct result of your actions. It's vital that you acknowledge those missteps and forgive yourself for them as forgiveness is an essential step to healing.

Forgiveness is for you

> *"Holding a grudge is like holding a Gun, with intentions of having someone Rest in Peace so why do you think they say*
>
> *'Speak now, or forever hold your, click click, piece'".*

A SMALL REMINDER FROM an excerpt from spoken word poem, Silence is Deadly. This poem confronts listeners to speak forgiveness even when it's difficult. We do not want to diminish the trauma endured by anyone reading this book. We understand that even while peering through some sections, you could have experienced triggers. But we must begin to understand the necessity of not only forgiving others that have offended us in our past bit developing a heart of forgiveness.

"If we fail to forgive our brothers and sisters then our God in Heaven will not forgive us."

Mark 11:25

Some people read this text and pass God off as being petty but we have to be able to consider the grave injustice. How is it fair that you're holding an offender hostage in your heart for their sins against you but you expect our Righteous judge to continue to willingly forgive you. The effort it takes to hold on to bitterness and resentment towards a person is exhausting. You weren't meant to bear that type of weight on your soul, it will eat away at the freedom God created you for. Spiritually you will suffer from your lack of forgiveness but even physically your body negatively responds to bitterness. The stress of these negative sentiments begin to affect blood pressure and nerves. Your body is literally crying out for you to forgive, and you need to listen, for your own sake. But you may say, how can I forgive someone who wasn't sorry for what they did, or if I come back into their lives to forgive them they will hurt me again. The truth is, you're not forgiving them for their sake, it's for yours, you're releasing your heart from bondage. Forgiveness doesn't require an apology. Your forgiveness is not an invitation for them into your heart, it's most often a gentle eviction from your heart. You're in essence saying, "I'm freeing myself from you, and you no longer have reign over my capacity to love." Reconciliation is always the goal, and it's a blessing when it happens however some cases may not give enough room for reconciliation. For example, if you were sexually abused as a child, it may not always be safe to bring this person around especially if you have children. Or if being around this person is a danger to your safety and those around you it's not wise to compromise your life and well-being to free yourself through forgiveness. Frankly, forgiveness does not even require them to be present, it must happen within.

You must uncover why you have difficulty with forgiving others. We assume it's not because you're not as nice as others or that the offenses against you have been greater. There has been something corrupting your 'God lens'. You've been viewing your situations through broken lenses. The only way to maintain a Godly perspective is to adopt God's heart towards his people. This is done by getting to know him better through his word.

How we view ourselves is critical because it affects how we interact with others and the world. Knowing that you have value and are worthy of love will help you to adopt and maintain a mindset that will bring love into your life. Remember that no one can truly love you if you don't first love yourself.

How We View Our Environment and Internalize Stimuli

WE VIEW OUR OBJECTIVE world through subjective lenses that are the product of our past experience. From our upbringing to past relationships, these experiences form biases that shape our view of the world and drive how we feel about it. We all have biases and they cause us to react in ways that are in line with our values and beliefs. For instance, an animal lover is much more likely to be affected by those sad advertisements of dogs in the pound than someone who doesn't care for animals. Knowing how certain external stimuli affect you is a huge step in healing past trauma and preventing future issues with both yourself and others.

Gratitude

VIEWING LIFE WITH GRATITUDE allows us to see the beauty in all things. This is because gratitude focuses us on what we have instead of what we lack. As humans, we tend to naturally focus on the negative.

This is a survival instinct as early man had to be able to quickly detect and avoid danger. Ironically, with issues like low self-esteem and brokenness (due to unfulfilled needs), we still take up a similar response of avoiding (and even denying) the necessary reaction of addressing the negative feelings we experience; all while failing to remove our focus from the negative feelings themselves. So, we continue to react based on the negative experiences, but do not confront them with a solution.

We would equate this to denying that our funds are low for the sake of spending as lavishly as usual. But then, suffering from the anxiety that continually eats at us whenever financial matters are brought to our attention. When living check to check and struggling to pay off each new bill is the norm, it would be sensible to stop creating or adding to our bills and expenses. But, we would first need to address that it is an issue, if there is to be any hope for resolution.

When it comes to gratitude, the practice itself isn't difficult; especially when life is going our way. But how do we maintain a positive and grateful mindset when we face hardship? First, we must recognize that hardship is a natural result of our imperfect world. Sin has separated us from God's full and perfect glory. Thus, we must toil. It sounds a bit pessimistic, but remember that God blessed us with the resilience to overcome obstacles and the intelligence to learn from them (we might even go so far as to argue that this was another way in which God made us in His image). Though painful, we must remember that setbacks are opportunities to learn and grow. Treating them as such, will weaken their power over us and aid in turning a trial into a triumph.

Additionally, it should be noted that as much as we all think we'd love to have a life with nothing to do—instead of being stuck in your day job—having that kind of lifestyle can eventually become very boring and dull. Without any particular focus or obligations, it's not hard to find yourself glued to a couch, bored out of your mind, while your television watches you. So, for the time being, we'd invite you to focus more closely on the reasons you are grateful for having a place to contribute your services in exchange for financial reward (insert wink here).

G.I. to IT

OUR BROTHER, BRANDON, is no stranger to hardship. He spent over twelve years in the Army serving all over the country as well as in both Iraq and Afghanistan. Long hours, arduous training, and time away from family defined a large part of his military career. Still, he loved it. He'd joined while still in high school and had excelled; quickly progressing in rank. At age 29, he'd just completed a successful command and was well on his way to a promotion. But while serving in Kuwait, Brandon began to experience double vision, impaired speech, and disorientation. After being convinced to go to the hospital to receive an MRI, Brandon received the heartbreaking news. He had Multiple Sclerosis. A rare autoimmune disorder, MS causes the immune system to attack and damage the brain. The results vary widely and can range from speech and vision impairment to full paralysis.

This diagnosis hit hard as it not only had implications on his long-term health, but it effectively ended his military career. The following year was filled with hardship and uncertainty. After his initial treatment proved ineffective, Brandon's condition worsened, spreading to his lower body and causing partial paralysis to his legs. To make matters worse, despite his best efforts, he was having difficulty finding a job. With the stress of his worsening condition and the fear of not being able to provide for his family, Brandon faced a mountain of challenges. However, throughout the process, he kept a smile on his face and gratitude in his heart.

"As crazy as it sounds, I think I'm one of the better people to have this disease. I have the love of my family, the support of my friends, the help of the military, and the knowledge that God will get us through this. There are a lot of people out there with far less and I'd rather I be in this situation than them."

Focusing on what he had instead of what he lacked helped Brandon to remain positive through an incredibly difficult time. That positivity has led him down a path that he says is better than the one he was traveling. After finding a treatment that is considerably more effective, his condition has improved and he is able to walk with less difficulty. He has transitioned from the military into the world of IT and works as a Project Manager for a large IT company. This has allowed him to spend more time at home with his family and to pursue his passion: writing. To learn more about Brandon's story and to connect with him, we've provided his contact information in the back of this book.

Another powerful purpose that setbacks and trials serve is to set us on the path God intended for us. In many cases, those who are lost, don't know it. Worst, some of us don't want to admit we are lost. But instead of wasting time wandering the proverbial desert, we can find purpose and truly live. A setback or hardship can block a potentially destructive path, forcing us onto the one that leads to prosperity. And so all experiences can serve us in some way if our mind is more focused on gratitude for the experience and if we stop to ask questions like, "How can that serve me?" and "What lesson can I pull from what just happened?"

When you encounter a tough time, it's important to avoid self-pity. But it's equally important to acknowledge your feelings and recognize them for what they are. We are not advocating suppressing your feelings or ignoring them. Instead, look at your feelings more critically and try to understand the root of those feelings. Knowing why we feel a certain way is incredibly helpful in a relationship because it aids us in communicating those feelings to our partner.

Hardship and Grief

SOME HARDSHIPS ARE exceptionally challenging, and hit us at our very core. The loss of a serious relationship or loved one can significantly alter our lives and set us on a potentially deadly path. Healing from loss and trauma can be a long and perilous journey and it's vital to ensure we pack light. Every unresolved issue in our life is weight we must carry. With each issue, the weight becomes heavier, slowing us down and eventually crushing us if we don't address it. The best way to initially address loss is allowing ourselves to grieve. All too often, we try to remain "strong" by stuffing our feelings into a box and hiding them away. But grieving is natural; more than that, it's healthy. Allowing yourself to experience all the emotions that come with a loss or trauma will allow you to move forward in the grieving process.

How We Think (Our Inner Voice)

Dealing with Doubt

> "And when he had entered, he said to them, 'Why are you making a commotion and weeping? The child is not dead but sleeping.' And they laughed at him. But he put them all outside and took the child's father and mother and those who were with him and went in where the child was. Taking her by the hand he said to her, 'Talitha cumi,' which means, 'Little girl, I say to you, arise.' And immediately the girl got up and began walking"

> *Mark 5:38-42*

ABOVE WE SEE A PICTURE of doubt clearly being dealt with by Jesus in scripture. The ruler and the people he had around him had their diagnosis of the situation; that situation was a dead daughter. Jesus, saw differently because he actually had the power to change the scenario. But before he spoke life into this girl, He swiftly moved all of the doubters out of the room. Jesus spends a lot of time teaching his disciples the power of belief and the danger of doubt. The conducive environment for the miraculous in this moment was a room where only belief existed. This scene teaches us how to invite change into our lives. To truly view things through our new God lenses we must learn to fully trust and believe Him. We can easily say we believe God but doubt shows up in our actions. After reading this book, we want you to walk in your new-found wholeness but you have to believe it. The best way to keep your life fit for change is by removing all mindsets, words and even people in your space that are perpetuating the dead ways you've known. Align yourself with a mindset and words that support the forgiven, delivered and healed *you*. Belief in God is quite radical, and just like the ruler's daughter that came back to life, once you rid doubt from your environment you are welcoming the miraculous hand of God for healing and restoration.

Our thoughts are powerful. They are the difference between us living a purpose filled life and living a life riddled with stagnation and regret. Thoughts drive actions, yet the energy needed to generate thoughts is finite. This is why having mental discipline in our everyday lives is critical. We cannot devote our mental and emotional energy to everything we encounter. However, all too often, we find ourselves getting upset about things that only matter in the moment; or worse, don't matter at all. How many times have you gotten upset about someone cutting you off on the highway (only to still end up at the same place at roughly the same time anyway)? How often does a coworker's attitude drive you to silent fury?

Feeling annoyed or even upset in the moment is natural but where it gets dangerous is when we put more thought and emotion into it than warranted. Some of us let these minor issues ruin our day, dwelling on them so heavily that we are unable to focus on anything else. These annoyances can compound until we are outright angry. This may be an extreme example but the same thing can happen in relationships. Perhaps a partner or person you've dated has said something that has upset you or that you didn't agree with. Instead of addressing it, you held onto it; allowing the dynamic to shift between you and souring your interaction. This is quite destructive in relationships as it can lead to fighting and passive aggressive behavior. The sad part is that these minor issues can be easily resolved if addressed immediately. However, just as we assign too much importance to the driver who cut us off, we assign extra weight to the issue we have with our partner. We mentally turn it into something that we feel is too big to solve with a simple conversation instead letting it reside in our mind and be fed by our negative emotions. Much like with the driver, we waste our day being upset; precious time that we have with our partner. The damage is two-fold though because we've not only made ourselves more upset than needed, but we've potentially done damage to the relationship.

"If everything is a priority, nothing is a priority"

Do you have a friend who is really high strung and seems to stress about everything? Are you perhaps that friend? There are things in our lives that require a significant amount of our energy and attention. Likewise, there will be far less important things that will still vie for that same energy and attention. We must be selective in what we give that finite energy to. Otherwise, we will be overwhelmed by a constant state of stress. So how do we ensure we avoid this? We focus on what really matters. Most of us don't realize this but there are really only a handful of things that truly matter in our lives. Some examples include: our relationship with God, family, friends and of course our purpose. All relationships and even visions that God give are simply opportunities for stewardship. They don't just sit and flourish, they require intentional time and effort to cultivate. Remember that the source of your joy and bounty from which all good things come is God. When you are sensitive to that relationship and prioritize it, your other areas of focus thrive from the spillover of your most important relationship. But things can become imbalanced when your priorities are out of whack. You can spend so much energy on your purpose that your loved ones feel trampled upon. This is why your relationship with God is so important, devotion to His word will make you aware or better yet a constant blessing to those he's called to be in your life.

In the end, when choosing what to focus our energy on we must ask ourselves three questions:

Does this issue really matter to me, and why?

Is the energy and attention cost of focusing on this issue acceptable?

Will focusing on this issue lead to true joy in my life?

We are not advocating caring about nothing or being numb because that can be just as destructive as caring about everything. What we encourage you to do is strike a balance between the two. Lock in on your priorities, activate your focus there. Make that a focal point in your life and give only as much energy as is absolutely required to everything else.

Staying in engaged with our priorities motivates us. One good friend told me, your motive is your motor. Your why keeps you going, but if your motive or your reasons are weak, your motor will fail. Motivation is important because it drives us forward even when we feel like turning back.

Biases

ANOTHER FACTOR THAT plays a significant part in how we think is the set of biases that we each hold. A bias is a prejudice against or preference toward one thing over another. They are a result of several factors including our language, culture, upbringing, and past experience. We all possess biases and they are not themselves bad. The danger comes in when we allow our biases to interfere with how we relate to other people and the world around us. God has charged us with loving one another and considering the needs of our brothers and sisters in Christ. Developing self-awareness regarding our biases will help us to live life as a whole individual with a healthy worldview. If we know what our biases are and how they influence us, we can take them into consideration when we feel particularly emotional about a specific issue. This will help us to check our emotions and determine if we are acting based on the actual issue or based on a bias. It will also help us to keep an open mind; allowing for more effective communication.

When hearing an opinion that conflicts with our own, it is easy to feel as if our opinion or belief is being attacked. This causes us to become defensive, walling ourselves off to the other person. However, hearing an opinion counter to your own does not invalidate yours; nor is their opinion any less valid. Recognizing that we all have biases and working within ourselves to keep them from limiting our perception of the world and how we relate to others will improve our thought processes as well as open us to greater possibilities.

How We Are Sustained

Do you not know that your bodies are temples of the Holy Spirit, who is in you, whom you have received from God? You are not your own

1 Corinthians 6:18-19

THROUGHOUT THIS CHAPTER, we've discussed our first fold of existence, consumption, as it pertains to how we process what enters into our bodies and minds. Managing how the outside world affects our inner selves is helpful in ensuring we maintain a healthy mindset, but this can be a taxing process. This is why we must also take actions to control what enters our body and mind when possible. Consumption begins with actual consumption so ensuring we maximize the beneficial elements while limiting the harmful ones will go a long way in helping us maintain a positive path. The body is indeed a temple for the Holy Spirit but we will go a step further. To us, the whole person (that is the body, mind, and spirit) is a machine; one that requires constant sustenance to maintain operation. Like any machine, it is a "garbage in, garbage out" setup. If we consume poor materials, we will yield poor products and our performance will be subpar. Your body and mind will still process the unsatisfactory materials that you give it, but it is only a matter of time before you will start to break down. Perhaps you already feel broken down after a lifetime of consuming subpar materials. The blessing is that humans are adaptive, and healing is possible.

So how do you keep the machine that is you running at maximum efficiency? Let's begin with maintenance. We hear a lot about self-care today; mostly on social media and in advertising. But beyond having a spa day or doing yoga, what does self-care really mean? Self-care has different meanings to different people but in general it is taking and active and deliberate role in one's own physical mental, emotional and spiritual health. It is being proactive and not waiting for a problem to arrive to address a health concern. It is taking steps to prevent health issues through living a healthy and happy life. In essence, it's the root of positive consumption.

So, how do we practice self-care? It begins with understanding which actions help us to be our best. This begins with the source. We all hate seeing that empty battery icon in the top corners of our phones. But we all know the longer we keep it off the charger it's only a matter of time before it dies. We should view our sustenance in the same way. God is our source of strength, joy, peace and love, the longer we stay disconnected it's only a matter of time before something dies on our lives. Staying plugged in looks like spending carved out time with him in prayer and his word. Sometimes it's as simple as sitting quietly, listening to sermons that charge you, pondering on His goodness and even singing sweet songs of worship. It's life changing to be a part of a church community that cares for your soul. It makes it easier to fellowship with friends who have a passion for the things of God as well, who nurture and give accountability to the renewed version of you. Some of you may not have friends of this sort, we implore you seek to make new friends. Surround yourself with people that live a life that build themselves and those around them. Even beyond your church community, find activities that improve your emotional, physical, or spiritual wellness.

These things will not just come to you, you have to initiate them. Stop sitting around waiting on God! He's waiting for you to take advantage of what he's made available to you!

Our fast-paced society leads us to believe we are too busy or committed to take out time for ourselves. However, the truth is that we give time to things we find important in the moment; which usually translates to things that can most effectively grab our attention.

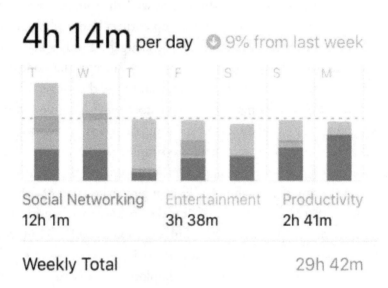

4h 14m per day ○ 9% from last week

T   W   T   F   S   S   M

Social Networking   Entertainment   Productivity
12h 1m   3h 38m   2h 41m

Weekly Total   29h 42m

One Writer's Phone Time Over a One Week Period

SCHEDULING TIME FOR self-care and sticking to that schedule will help us hold ourselves accountable for spending our time in a way that benefits our overall health. The positive stimuli from this is fuel for the machine that is you, and it will help you to feel more refreshed before taking on more of life's repeated or new challenges.

Self-care is not just about planning isolated activities that you enjoy. It is a lifestyle change that involves focusing on your overall wholeness, wellness, and health. Healthy daily habits play a significant part in this. Even in its resting state, the brain consumes about 20% of the body's energy. This means the brain is constantly finding ways to save energy and remain efficient. The brain naturally gravitates toward activities that are familiar because they require less thought and are thus more energy efficient. This is why it is vital to develop habits that aid in a healthy lifestyle instead of the occasional healthy activity.

"So, whether you eat or drink or whatever you do, do it all for the glory of God."

1 Corinthians 10:31

One set of habits that profoundly impacts our health in America specifically is our eating habits. What we consume fuels our journey and we want to ensure it is of high quality. Be it the taste, convenience, or some other appeal, fast food and junk food are killing us. According to the Centers for Disease Control, in 2015, the obesity rate in America was nearly 40%, affecting 93.3 million adults. Worse, this number was higher in Black and Hispanic populations (46.8% and 47% respectively). This is a clear indicator that we are not taking an active role in our health, instead taking this gift that God has given us for granted. Whether you fall into this category or not, being more mindful of the foods you eat and making healthier choices will benefit your physical, mental, and emotional health.

Along with diet, lack of exercise is a contributing factor to obesity and poor health in general. Now we are not here to tell you to get a gym membership or run a marathon. We are more interested in helping you recognize that the body needs physical activity and there are opportunities for it everywhere. Remember, loving yourself is more than a mindset. It's a deliberate set of actions to care for your body and mind. It all ties into wholeness through self-care. We are stewards of these bodies and minds that the Lord has given us and we are accountable to him for how we maintain them.

As we mentioned before we are strong believers in therapy. The same way a car goes in for a tune up every so often, and we also go in for medical checkups consistently throughout our lives, we should not ignore our mental checkups. We need to be held accountable that we are continuing to move in a healthy direction personally and relationally. Once you find a professional or spiritual counselor that helps you process your initial trauma and healing, we recommend you see them periodically to assess your growth or to help you tackle new issues that may arise.

It can be challenging to maintain healthy habits; especially when we are surrounded by crutches. A crutch is anything that provides temporary support to us when we are having difficulty. It can range from an item like food or drugs to an activity like shopping. browsing social media, or sex. Like the medical device, crutches are intended for temporary use. However, we become accustomed to leaning on crutches instead of relying on our own abilities. Because crutches are often tied to negative habits, it is necessary to avoid them to prevent relapsing into our old ways. Ultimately, crutches give us a temporary boost but the feeling doesn't last. Worse, the more we use them to distract ourselves from real issues, the more we need to.

It may seem impossible to develop a mindset that leads you to a path of consistently healthy choices but it benefits you to live with the mindset that you were built for more. You are too valuable to run God's temple into the ground, take control of your health or sickness will take control of you.

God Wants YOU to Take Initiative

OUR BROTHER, MILAN, is no stranger to pursuing fitness or clean eating. In fact, he's the one who is always advising us on many of the best foods to eat or avoid for things like weight loss, mental clarity, better energy, and overall good health.

But, for much of his early life, his eating habits were about as bad as many of his peers. Highly sweetened, processed, and inflammatory foods were a staple of his diet. And even though he often made an effort to take in a serving or two of veggies, it wasn't nearly enough to make up for his regularly bad eating habits. Most of us assume that this is something we can ignore as long as we're in decent physical shape. And so did Milan. He was a personal trainer, an athlete, and it wasn't at all uncommon for others to ask him how he remained so fit.

But despite all of his training and consistent exercise, his diet eventually started to affect his blood pressure. It began to show just as he was transitioning from junior college into a university. He went in for a routine physical, and the doctor noted his blood pressure was elevated. He advised that Milan watch his salt intake, and keep an eye on his blood pressure through regular checkups.

Milan initially took the advice lightly, believing that as long as he exercised enough and drank more water, his blood pressure was bound to go back to normal in no time. But a few months later, Milan went to the school nurse one day, thinking to get his blood pressure checked on a whim. And he got quite the surprise. His blood pressure had shot up. He'd been eating worse since starting at his university, partially out of desire to experience the freedom of adulthood. But his eating was also the result of his ever-growing stressful financial woes that came with having to take on far more student loans than he was comfortable with; all for the sake of furthering his education.

He tried to tell himself that he could cut back on desserts and fast food, but the rise in his blood pressure made it clear that his efforts weren't enough. Despite how often everyone else told him he *looked* fine, he certainly didn't feel fine. Over the course of about three months, his blood pressure went higher and higher into dangerous readings until he was eventually placed on four different medications at once (consisting of a mixture of blood thinners and beta blockers).

Needless to say this was a tough hit for him, as he tried to apply the nutritional advice that his physicians and nurses offered. He drank more water and reduced his salt intake even further; desperate for a solution. But nothing seemed to help.

It had been nearly one year since he was diagnosed with hypertension and placed on medication, and nothing seemed to be working. He started to feel like he was trapped in a dark tunnel; asking why he of all his friends and family was suffering from a condition generally associated with elevated age and weight gain. But this didn't resolve the issue or provide him any settling answers. So, instead of complaining, he prayed. It was more than a little depressing being a college student in good physical shape, but still having high blood pressure. Milan was always the type of person that wanted to get to the bottom of things, and this situation was no different. He asked his primary physician and school nurses what tests could be conducted, and learned what he could from each of them. This consisted of blood and urine samples and even a renal angiogram (where a small camera at the end of a tube is inserted near the groin and tunneled up toward the kidneys to look for blockages).

But even after all these tests, no answers came. Milan wondered if there was ever to be any hope for improvement, or if he'd be stuck on medication for the rest of his life. But then, the first of two miracles happened thirteen months into his initial diagnosis.

His physicians were running their routine tests, and his blood pressure was lower. Much lower. In fact, it was almost back to normal. For the first time in a long time, Milan had hope. He no longer felt like he was stuck. Far from it. It was as though God had shined a light down the tunnel he'd been in, and Milan was determined to learn how to keep this light blazing brightly.

On one unexpected day, Milan was at a church conference where the pastor gave a blessing over the food, and during grace, the quote from Hippocrates vividly popped into Milan's mind. "Let food be thy medicine, and medicine thy food." In that moment, something clicked, and Milan was certain it was the answer to his prayers. Why hadn't he thought about it before? The answer should've been so simple.

Over the next few years, Milan dedicated a reasonable portion of his time and attention toward learning what kinds of foods most likely contributed to his hypertension and other conditions caused by excess inflammation within the human body. He still learns more even now, and has become a wealth of information over the years. But one lesson Milan has continued to live by was his realization that God has blessed us with both a curious mind and the determination to quell that curiosity with knowledge and wisdom. Wisdom that can help us to take better care of our minds and bodies. Wisdom that allows us to show Him gratitude for our bodies by treating them as the sacred temples that God made them to be.

It is through this knowledge (gathering information) and wisdom (learning to apply that information) that he's continued to learn and gained a handle on improving his health one food at a time. It's been more than twelve years since Milan's battle with high blood pressure. But thanks to better eating, and a mind rooted in gratitude for all that God has blessed him with, his blood pressure remains in a very healthy range, and he continues to find more reasons to smile every day. Just as we must be stewards of what we put into our minds, so must we be stewards of what we put into our bodies. It is one of our God-given responsibilities; which means we must not neglect or ignore it.

He now quotes other health books and nutrition gurus saying things like, "Everything you eat is either building your body up or breaking it down." But of all the sayings and quotes he's leaned on, we asked which one he leans on most. This was his answer:

> *"I believe that many people fail to understand the importance of using what God has given us to heal and improve ourselves and to help one another. We absolutely must take initiative for our own physical health. It is not up to our doctors and nurses to keep us healthy. It is each one of our personal responsibilities. Perhaps we should consider the financial and emotional costs we will pay on the back end, when we've worn this gift—our body—down. It can bankrupt us financially. And seeing how that will bring sadness to those who care about us—as we deteriorate right in front of them—can bankrupt our loved ones emotionally. Do they deserve that? Does anyone?"*

So, how can we use what we have, if we don't know how to use it—or that we're even supposed to use it? Hosea 4:6 says it best.

> *"My people are destroyed for lack of knowledge: because thou hast rejected knowledge, I will also reject thee, that thou shalt be no priest to me: seeing thou hast forgotten the law of thy God, I will also forget thy children."*

I don't know if the importance of pursuing the gift of knowledge and wisdom could be any clearer than that scripture. But as a child of God, it is very important to me.

A Note on Romance Media

MANY OF US GREW UP in broken homes and do not have a clear example of what a real loving relationship between a married couple looks like. Having not been taught this at home, we naturally seek out other sources to educate us. Many of us learned (and continue to learn) about romantic relationships through books, movies, and television.

What this did was create in us an expectation that is not fully rooted in reality. Romance media (like most media) is designed to be sensational. It is vying for our attention like everything else and must present the most interesting content possible. This means intense drama, passionate love scenes, and a perfect ending. For those of us who do not have a foundational understanding of how real relationships work, this can create unrealistic expectations. These isolated exaggerations put relationships in a funhouse mirror and distort our understanding of what real communication, intimacy, and sexuality look like. Real relationships are God ordained and require more nuance; they can't be conveniently wrapped up by the time the credits role. We are not saying that you should avoid this type of media. We simply want you to have an awareness of how it may affect you mentally, emotionally, and spiritually.

Summary

LIVING AS A MORE WHOLE person requires we live a more deliberate life. We must have an awareness of how we perceive our world and how it affects our psyche. In this chapter, we discussed the concept of consumption or what we put into ourselves. Our minds and bodies are in a constant state of consumption. Everything we take in subtly alters us. We have little control over how the things we consume affect our body. However, we can control how our mind processes certain stimuli and ultimately, the effect it has on us. To achieve this, we must have an understanding of four point-of-view actions:

- How we view ourselves
    - You have value; start by knowing your value and not discounting yourself
    - Forgive yourself for your past mistakes
    - You are beautiful; know that beauty is the sum of all aspects of a person (physical, mental, emotional,

spiritual)
- Celebrate the things you love about yourself while working to improve the things you feel need attention

- How we view our environment and internalize stimuli
  - We experience our objective world through subjective lenses
  - How we view our environment has a profound impact on how it affects us
  - Viewing the good with gratitude allows us to see the beauty in all things
  - Viewing setbacks as opportunities for growth (trials) helps us to remain positive through hardship
  - We shouldn't ignore the bad or but rather see it for what it is and find the good in it
  - Hardships affect us negatively and in these cases, we must allow ourselves to grieve

- How we think (our inner voice)
  - It's vital that we are selective in what we give our emotional energy to (it's finite)
  - We must strike a balance between caring about every little thing and caring about nothing
  - God is our source, we must stay connected and continue to affirm what he says about us
  - When faced with problems, we should focus on finding the solution instead of finding reasons to be upset about it
  - Our biases have a significant effect on our worldview and we must recognize what our biases are so that we don't succumb to the pitfalls associated with them

- How we are sustained
  - ○ Garbage in garbage out definitely applies
  - ○ Establish healthy daily habits and stick to them
  - ○ What we put in our bodies impacts us physically and emotionally
  - ○ Our activity level can affect our physical health, motivation, and emotional well-being
  - ○ Crutches give us an instant boost but don't last and the more we use them, the more we need; use them appropriately. Don't let them use you. Some you must let go. (food, shopping, drugs, alcohol, sex, social media)

- On Romance media
  - ○ They can create unrealistic expectations of relationships, intimacy, and sexuality
  - ○ They are designed to be sensational and are thus isolated exaggerations of what happens in real relationships
  - ○ But real relationships require far more nuance

Which of these four point-of-view actions do you feel is your greatest struggle right now?

———————

WHAT NEXT STEP(S) CAN you take to start (or continue) resolving your struggle with this action?

Chapter 5: The Prosperity of External Growth

———

This is where things start getting exciting. Just because you can't undo *what* has affected you doesn't mean you can't undo *how* it has affected you. Where you found yourself in chapter 3 you can be rescued here in chapter 5.

Dismantling Your Toxic Love Styles

Fearful Lover No More

THE CHALLENGE OF THE fearful lover is not necessarily boldness but surrender. Simply being okay with not being okay. The fearful lover walks into relationships ready to run away. Primed to escape uncertainty, sadness, incompetence but especially vulnerability. You're afraid to put yourself out there because you're afraid to break again. Here's the good news, and the guarantee. Discovering who you are and whose you are won't keep you from falling, but it will guarantee that the fall won't break you.

Stop running. You are free, to be uncertain, to be sad and to cry, to feel alone and hopeless. You are permitted to feel all of these things and actually communicate them

in a healthy way to a professional or the people that you love. You're especially free to talk to God about it. Admission of your weakness is a prerequisite for God to be strong in your life and remind you that even though you're uncertain, he holds your life in His hands. It's okay to cry as things can become more difficult than what you feel you're ready for. We know that weeping can endure for a night, but let us not forget that His joy will come in the morning. It's okay if you feel alone sometimes. But keep in mind that an empty room doesn't mean His presence has departed from you. God doesn't break promises, and He has already promised to never leave nor forsake us. You might think you're hopeless, but in Christ you have both your hope and your prize. He sacrificed so that—despite how dark— this world is not the finish line.

> *"For I reckon that the sufferings of this present time are not worthy to be compared with the glory which shall be revealed in us."*
>
> *Romans 8:18*

Insecure Lover Who?

YOU MUST UNDERSTAND insecurity has been tied to your identity like a fungus that has bound itself to every aspect of your being. So not only do you love yourself and others insecurely, you also may think, work and even play insecurely. The untangling of yourself from this toxic web can take time but it's possible.

There used to be talk shows that were popularized in the 1990's and early 2000's where guests on the show would bring on their friends or family members who dress and carry themselves in a way that (for lack of better terms) made them look plain and ugly. They would spend time with fashion, hair and make-up stylists and would get transformed. One of the first things these people would say when the makeover was done is, "I feel like a totally different person" and "I feel so much more confident!" While we do believe there is merit to this makeover process, we believe in a much more profound type of makeover. Before an inch of hair is cut curled or dyed, before a drop of makeup is added or an article of clothing is swapped. God desires to make you secure in Him first. Because he is the unmovable anchor. He calls you beautifully and wonderfully made. Not just outwardly but because of the spirit He breathed in you. You were made in his image and He makes no mistakes. You no longer have to settle for less than His best for your life. But you cannot be insecure in Him and have faith at the same time. Insecurity in God is essentially saying, I don't believe you are who you say you are. Be secure in His perspective of you, and His ability to keep you safe and comforted. Recognizing you're a child of God grants you the most solid basis for confidence, and assuredness because of whose you are.

Bye-Bye Selfish Lover

IT WASN'T SO NICE KNOWING ya' but it's time to part ways with this toxic trait of selfishness. When you truly realize your selfishness is a defense mechanism—a means to protect your heart from missing out on what you believe you deserve—it becomes easier to abandon this type of behavior. Your best answer to selfishness is gratitude. When you approach relationships with the notion that every part of it is a gift then you will better appreciate every unexpected phone call, every encouraging word, every genuine hug. Why? Because a pure expression of love is a sacrifice. It should be appreciated but not idolized. You have to continue to not only exhibit a character that attracts friendship and community but one that clearly communicates this in healthy ways. As a selfish lover you manipulated people to take what you wanted from them. But as a grateful lover you become and give what you desire from others.

Desperate Lover Never Again

WHILE WE STILL UPHOLD there is a virtue in having strong desire and willingness to go to great lengths for love, it must be understood that a relationship doesn't look like loving others at the detriment of yourself. A relationship is not supposed to destroy but rejuvenate you and remind you of the beauty in serving another person with pure intent. Although you may find yourself in situations where you are helping other people or enduring for the sake of their edification, when it comes to marriage, there is an expectation for mutual commitment and effort. Never again will you find yourself in a situation where you are pouring your life into someone while they are completely unresponsive No more will you sacrifice yourself at the feet of someone not willing to grow and invest in the relationship with you. You have to disconnect from the void created by the collapsed pillars of your childhood by recognizing how God has preserved you as well as your value. You should only be willing to surrender to love that honors Him first. Being desperate to the point of your destruction does not give God Glory. Growing in self sacrificial love for others and obedience to God is the goal.

Loving Your Offenders

WE CAN'T LET YOU CONTINUE to read this book and make you believe that there isn't any implication on those who got you here. We believe in reconciliation and restoration because at the end of the day, isn't that the heart of the Gospel? Sinful man—through Christ's death on the cross—is reconciled back to a Holy God.

In Chapter 2 we looked at the roots of brokenness and we saw how we may have lacked essential love pillars from our parents. Perhaps your parents are no longer alive. To be completely honest with you, you will have to learn to heal and grow independent of what they say or do. But wouldn't it be beautiful if you actually had an opportunity to help them see how you may have been affected by the way they raised you, and how you plan to take steps towards healing. This is not an easy thing to do, knowing that in most cases our parents did their best and never in a million years would have imagined that they would be partly responsible for the toxic behaviors we are attempting to heal from today. But sometimes it's not about what you say but how you say it.

Think about what you plan to say. Pray about it and how you desire for it to be received. You don't want your parents to feel attacked by your presentation but encouraged by your honesty and maturity. The scriptures also tells us that a soft answer turns away wrath. Approach them first with gratitude. Tell them extensively, how you appreciated the good things they did. If you don't have memories of such great efforts then thank them for being willing to listen to you in that moment. Then tell them a bit about what you've learned and how you think may have been affected by your shared past with them. You can also ask them questions about how they were raised and perhaps some of the ways their parents could have failed them. You may be surprised; this moment could turn into a rare moment of bonding and even an opportunity for growth and change for a parent who may have never even known of the things you will be sharing with them.

Be clear about one thing. You're not seeking for an apology. You're taking advantage of an opportunity for transparency and personal healing. You're also using this moment as an opportunity to close that chapter of your life; to cut the umbilical cord that tied you to past trauma and have a restored relationship with the human being(s) that brought you into this world.

Let It Go from a Distance

YOUR OFFENSE FROM THE past may have included someone who has now passed away. In a situation like this you must be willing to see your freedom not as something they could give, but as something you're giving yourself, but you're allowing them to witness the process. Let it go from where you are, your heart will recognize it.

There are some complicated scenarios where the offender involved was someone who violated you sexually as a child. We believe that wisdom should be considered here. We understand the difficulty involved in attempting to face your perpetrator. We've heard of people who have done it successfully. However, even if a past sexual predator is a family member, your safety should be taken in high regard. You don't want to be placed in a predicament where you begin to experience memory triggers or the offender is overcome with such embarrassment and guilt that they become aggressive in their denial. We feel it's more appropriate to let this go from

a distance. The incident(s) may forever be stained in your memory but it does not have to imprison your heart. You must believe that you were a victim of something cruel and perverted. But do not let your trauma teach you how to love or how to repel it. Rather let your new lenses help you see the purity of Agape love and strengthen your desire to pour it on others. Forgive your offender and pray that they come to an understanding of their actions and repent. Unfortunately, they were broken at one point but chose to cut you with their fragments. If you truly desire to get this weight off your chest. Find a counselor and share everything, the difficult parts and the ugly parts. Or write a letter to the person. Write everything you won't have an opportunity to say face to face, you can choose to burn or bury the letter or if you give to the person if you feel led to. But do not let it burn or bury you. Release yourself from the bondage of past abuse. And do not wait for nor expect their apology because it doesn't carry your healing. God has given you everything you need to be whole.

Being Married is a Blessing Not the Goal

WE WANT TO MAKE IT clear that although we are grateful for our marriage and encourage people all around to embrace the beauty and gift of matrimony, it is not the answer to your problems. We want you to see that God has made you a gift to your family, workplace and community at large. As Christians, we do a bad job of showing single people that they can be whole as they are. God can get glory from your life, and you can enjoy the goodness of life without having a spouse. Wedding bells are a blessing that comes with its own challenges. The scripture tells us, to whom much is given much is required. Having another heart to steward is "much". Though rewarding, a good marriage is lifelong path of self-sacrifice and work. Don't force yourself into a relationship because it is over glorified. It's not the cure for brokenness and God can still use your singleness to bless many.

Keys for a Prosperous Relationship

A LARGE PART OF LIVING as a more whole person is about our interactions with other people.

God has given us His spirit to enable us to have successful relationships. In Galatians 5:22 Paul tells us:

> "But the fruit of the Spirit is love, joy, peace, patience, kindness, goodness, faithfulness, gentleness, self-control; against such things there is no law."

Living with these fruit active pushes us to be more focused on others. Being able to look outside of ourselves and understand the people around us will make a significant difference in our lives. When fruit show up in our lives, there are 'musts' that will remain constant:

- You must view life as collaboration and not a competition
- You must try to view issues from the perspective of the other person
- You must exemplify the qualities you want to attract
- You must understand that no one is perfect
- You must know that great communication leads to a great relationship

> "And let us consider how to stir up one another to love and good works, not neglecting to meet together, as is the habit of some,

but encouraging one another, and all the more as you see the Day drawing near."

Hebrews 10:24-25

View Life as a Collaboration and Not a Competition

RESOURCES ARE FINITE. There is only so much food, so many jobs, so many suitable mates, and so many adequate places to live. While this is a fact of life, this does not mean there aren't enough resources to go around. Still, we see so many people treating life like it's a competition. They hoard resources and information for fear that helping others will somehow hurt them. Perhaps you have a coworker who refuses to help out around your job because they want to be the only one who looks good around the boss. Perhaps you have a family member who is miserly because they think sharing their wealth will cause them to go broke overnight. This thought process of one must lose for another to gain is all too common and can be the unfortunate result of past trauma.

"Let each of you look not only to his own interests, but also to the interests of others."

Philippians 2:4

Competition is healthy, but overly competitive people can view relationships as a zero-sum game. This term, which is common in financial theory, illustrates a situation in which there can be no net gain among participants meaning that a gain for one participant results in an equal loss for the other. In this, there is no victory without defeat, no gain without loss. This makes sense in the financial world, but it can be highly destructive in our relationships, work, and family life.

It's not to say that there are not people out there who also have this mindset and will try to take all they can from you. But as Christians, our charge is to love and support one another. A collaborative spirit will draw people to you because humans are social creatures that naturally want to work together. At work, if you are known as a team player, coworkers will appreciate your willingness to help out and your boss may even take notice. Leaders look out for the welfare of the team and we don't have to be in a leadership position to lead.

The place where understanding this concept is most effective is in dating and relationships. Dating has changed over the past decades with the rise of online dating and dating apps. With unprecedented access to potential mates, the dating process has become very impersonal. People can shop for a date as easily as they shop for a car; filtering by size, color, and model year. Because matching, messaging and going out is so easy, it can give people a false sense of importance and entitlement. We've interviewed men and women who have been on multiple dates a week with no clear purpose in mind. This type of exploration is a bit excessive as it can keep interactions shallow because both people know that they can be replaced. This makes it difficult for people to invest in one another and can even make interactions hostile. No one wants to give emotionally for fear of losing a part of themselves to the other person.

Online dating cannot be solely to blame for this issue however. As we mentioned earlier, in relationships, even marriages, there can be a toxic mindset that one person must win and the other must lose. This is especially prevalent in an argument where each person is trying to make their point. What many do not realize is that usually when one person wins, both people lose. Yes, you've made your point and tasted the sweet victory of being right, but what type of damage have you done to your relationship by verbally beating the other person into submission? This is why dating and relationships must be collaborative just like in a work environment. The stakes are too high for it not to be.

In the case of dating, it shouldn't matter who is paying or what movie you go see. You are both there to get to know each other and see if you can form a connection (at least, you should be). Everything else is secondary. Adopting this mindset and letting it show through your actions can not only be liberating, but it can be encouraging to the other person who may then let down their defenses. As we discussed in chapter 4, you have a finite amount of energy. Focus it on what is most important and let the rest fall into place.

When looking at some of the hardest aspects of dating in today's society, we found that the mindset of many would-be daters out there has a lot to do with their general feelings of difficulty with dating as a whole. So, we've compiled a short list of a few ideas to keep in mind while dating. If you even remotely identify with any of these, we invite you to take a closer look at yourself and ask how this behavior might be negatively impacting your experience with others.

Dating Pitfalls:

1. Being too self-absorbed and desperate to fit in with your friends and peers; as if their approval is more important than God's
2. Not being willing to put in the same effort as the other person (treat dating like you're just along for the ride)
3. Feeling like you don't have to express gratitude for the kindness the other person shows
4. Being more focused on what the person you're dating can do for you than what you can do together
5. Wanting the other person to accept you for who you are (especially your flaws) while heavily judging him
6. Being too closed off emotionally and imposing negative past experiences on new people
7. Being too emotionally available too quickly

8. Willingness to compromise morals for the possibility of companionship

9. Having unrealistic expectations and having a cookie cutter idea of the perfect man

Let us remember that relationships are a collaboration from day one. Two whole people coming together with an open heart and mind have the potential to build something incredible. Unlike in a zero-sum game where resources are fixed, in relationships, participants can pool resources to obtain more resources. Whether it's something financial like buying a house together or something intangible like building an emotional sanctuary for one another, relationships allow us to transcend our limits as individuals. The beauty of a relationship is that we can create something new that we would not be able to create on our own. This requires us to be wise but open, to trust, and have a collaborative spirit. We can both win if we work together.

Try to View Issues from the Perspective of the Other Person

IN PHILIPPIANS 2:4 the church is encouraged to:

"Let each of you look not only to his own interests, but also to the interests of others".

This principle does wonders in conflict resolution. Viewing an issue from the perspective of the person you are in conflict with is an effective way to better understand their position and drive toward a solution. If our ultimate goal is to achieve victory together, then it is necessary for us to understand what victory means to all parties. Doing this requires us to develop empathy.

"If one member suffers, all suffer together; if one member is honored, all rejoice together."

1 Corinthians 12:26

Most of us are familiar with sympathy in which we feel sorrow or pity for the hardship or trials that other experience. However, empathy takes this to the next level. When you are empathetic toward someone, you are attempting to feel what they feel, putting yourself in their shoes. Empathy is powerful when trying to relate to someone who is experiencing a difficult time but it can be just as beneficial in everyday interactions. Understanding and considering the feelings of others places us in a unique position to meet their needs. We all have a problem we are seeking to solve when we interact with someone; whether it's two coworkers trying to complete a project on time, a couple arguing over finances, or two friends chatting to pass the time. Identifying and understanding the other person's problem helps us to orient the conversation toward the solution and communicate in a way that drives toward the solution.

We all want to be understood and people generally want to talk to us; we just have to invite them to talk. How do we do this? Ask questions and listen; actively. Fight the urge to rebut or add your two cents. Just let them talk. Try to avoid thinking about what you are going to say next since we can easily miss key information from one another when our minds are more focused on preparing a rebuttal. Despite what you may have been led to believe, multi-tasking is virtually impossible for our brain to do efficiently. Trying to place significant focus on two tasks (which require our undivided attention) at once is like trying to walk left and right at the same time. The brain cannot do it. It also helps us to avoid premature judgment of what the person is saying.

If you start placing more concentration on simply hearing the other person's words you will be astonished at how much more you can learn about them. You may even get the coveted "you're a really good listener" or "you're really easy to talk to" award. A word of caution on this though. Be willing to offer your feelings and thoughts when the time comes. A conversation is an exchange after all. Adopting the other person's perspective helps us view the world through different lenses enabling us to better relate to those we interact with.

Exemplify the Qualities You Want to Attract

HAVING PLEASING INTERACTIONS with those around us is great, but in many cases, we want to attract people who we can build meaningful long-term relationships with. If you are happy with the friends you have and are in a happy committed relationship, this section may be a bit of a review for you. But if you are looking to find new friends or a new romantic partner, you may find this helpful. Finding people who mesh with you is as simple as exhibiting the qualities of the person you want to attract. All too often, we hide aspects of ourselves for fear that we won't be accepted. Whether it's our nerdy tendencies, our love of gardening, or even our relationship with Christ, we avoid being ourselves because we fear the judgment of others. Meanwhile, we wonder why we can't find that person who has those qualities we are looking for.

The truth is that this person we are searching for could be overlooking us because they don't see those qualities in us that would attract them; despite the fact that we possess them. What you project will affect people's perception of you and will attract or repel them based on how your projection resonates with them. Want to keep negative people out of your life? Be overwhelmingly positive. Misery loves company and complainers will get tired of complaining around you if you don't feed their negativity. The same goes for positive people. Most people in a good mood don't want to be brought down so projecting a positive presence will attract and hold positive people. If you expect a Godly man, present yourself as a Godly woman. Our ideal person is out there but we must be prepared to receive and care for them.

Understand That No One is Perfect

UNDERSTANDING THAT no one is perfect and reconciling that with our expectations is perhaps the most challenging aspect of finding and building a relationship with someone. We have in our heads the image of an ideal person, an ideal relationship, and an ideal life. Unfortunately, when potential mates fail to live up to our ideal image, we quickly disqualify them. On the other end of the spectrum are those of us who believe we'll never find our ideal mate so we don't even try; instead taking the first person to come along who seems halfway decent. Both are harmful because we are not focused on finding the mate that God has chosen for us. The root of this issue is the coveted and dreaded checklist. From early childhood, we begin to form views of how a healthy relationship should look. These views are heavily influenced by our observation of parental figures. However, as we mentioned earlier in chapter 4, there is often an absence of these positive relationships. Many of us did not have both parents in the home or if we did, their relationship exemplified qualities that we would rather avoid. Because of this, it fell to television, movies, and the internet to teach us what a meaningful relationship looked like. This created and reinforced delusions of a perfect person whom we could live happily ever after with. From this delusion, many of us have created a checklist that we use to assess our compatibility with potential mates.

While there is an ideal person who God has prepared for each of us, that person is not perfect. Checklists tend to hold potential mates to unrealistic standards making it impossible to connect with anyone who doesn't check all boxes. The reality is that finding and connecting with our ideal person will likely require that some boxes remain unchecked. We are not suggesting you lower your standards; they exist to keep you from settling for someone not suited for you. We instead encourage you to rethink how you assess potential mates by considering God's purpose in bringing men and women together.

"But for Adam, no suitable helper was found. So the Lord God caused the man to fall into a deep sleep; and while he was sleeping, he took one of the man's ribs and then closed up the place with flesh. Then the Lord God made a woman from the rib he had taken out of the man, and he brought her to the man. The man said, "This is now bone of my bones and flesh of my flesh she shall be called 'woman,' for she was taken out of man.' That is why a man leaves his father and mother and is united to his wife, and they become one flesh."

Genesis 2:20-24

Long before you were born, God had in mind the person who would connect you to that would give Him glory. We cannot use our mate to supplement our brokenness, but must come together as two whole beings who would give God more Glory than they could individually. This is encouraging because it means that a loving and fulfilling relationship was promised by God. We just have to take the necessary actions to prepare ourselves to receive this gift.

Spheres of Attraction

RECOGNIZING AND UNITING with our mate requires that we approach our assessment of potential love interests a bit differently. This is where a method we call Spheres of Attraction comes into play. We mentioned earlier that having a checklist can be counterproductive as it makes disqualifying potential mates extremely easy. Spheres of Attraction does not reject the checklist but reworks it to help us better grasp what is most important to us.

Imagine you are on your own little planet; we will use Dana as an example. The planet represents Dana as a person; her goals, dreams, thoughts, and attitudes. Now imagine there are objects orbiting around this planet that have varying effects on it. Immediately surrounding the planet is faith which serves as its atmosphere so to speak. Closest in orbit to the planet are values. A bit further out are guiding principles. Furthest out are behaviors.

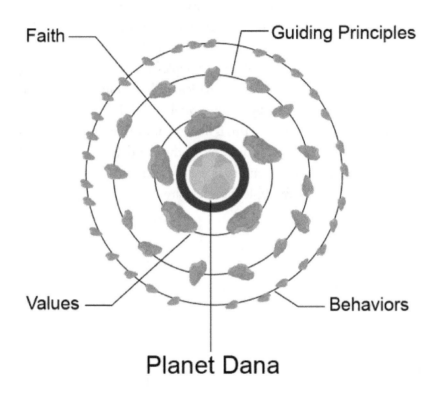

FAITH SURROUNDS PLANET Dana, encapsulating it like our own atmosphere. Everything she experiences is viewed through the lens of faith and it is core to her being. Our faith affects all that we do and is essential in forming our value system. When looking for a mate, faith is of paramount importance. Having a working interfaith relationship is not impossible, but considering how important your faith is, it is unlikely that God would place someone of a conflicting faith in your romantic path. The scripture tells us to not be unequally yoked to an unbeliever so much prayer and consideration must come to play when it comes to examining the person you intend to spend the rest of your life with.

Values are closest in orbit to Planet Dana and have the greatest effect on her outside of faith. They are the largest items because they are the most important to her, being a fundamental part of who she is. Values are developed over extended periods of time and are core aspects of our personality. They drive our guiding principles and behaviors and along with faith, form the foundation on which we build our identity. Items within this sphere are usually non-negotiable and if they do not align with a potential mate's values, this is likely an indicator that a long-term relationship will not work. This is due to the fact that mismatched value systems can make it difficult to make life decisions that both parties are comfortable with. Examples of values are:

Honesty

Loyalty

Respect

Open-mindedness

Compassion

Discipline

Humor

Selflessness

Guiding principles are outside of the values sphere but still hold significance. They are thought processes that have been engrained over time and drive behaviors. They are somewhat difficult to change as people tend to invest a significant amount of energy into them. Like faith and values, they have a significant effect on one's personality and attitudes toward the world. Since guiding principles sprout from values, people tend to have more guiding principles. A mismatch of guiding principles is not necessarily a relationship death sentence but it is an indicator that more work is required to make a relationship mesh. Examples of guiding principles are:

Life is a gift, don't waste it

The sour truth is better than a sweet lie

Everything is worth trying once

We were placed in this world to serve others

God has a plan for us all

Humor is the antidote of despair

Furthest from Planet Dana and by far the most plentiful are behaviors. Influenced by guiding principles, behaviors are simply our actions. They are relatively easy to change if someone really wants to change them and in some cases can be overlooked depending on how detrimental they are to the relationship. These are often used as disqualifiers but it's important to avoid judging a person solely on their behaviors. Behaviors do point to guiding principles however so a significant collection of undesirable behaviors can mean there is a mismatch of guiding principles. A few examples of behaviors are:

Being blunt in conversation

Remaining calm during challenging situations

Joking during stressful situations

Eating healthy

Shutting down after correction

Obsession with proving a point

Procrastination

Being kind to others

If you notice, we can take these example behaviors and trace a path back to the example values. It also does not hurt to ask potential mates what guides them as well as what they value and see how their behavior aligns with this. Most importantly, examining your own values and connecting them to your guiding principles and behaviors will give you a solid assessment of who you are and what you will want to look for in a mate.

Keep in mind that within each sphere, some items are more important than others. A potential mate can still be disqualified if certain behaviors deeply affect you in a negative way. It is also important to ensure that your faith, values, and guiding principles shine through in your behavior. If you value compassion, you must be compassionate. If respect matters to you, strive to treat everyone with respect. This goes back to being the type of person you want to attract. However, beyond that, it is about being true to yourself in thought and action. If you are to unite with the person God has made for you, it is vital that you recognize one another.

> *"Be completely humble and gentle; be patient, bearing with one another in love."*
>
> *1 Peter 4:8*

Trust, But Verify

ON YOUR JOURNEY THROUGH life, you will likely encounter people who seek to take advantage of your kindhearted nature. Perhaps you already have and this has contributed to your brokenness. It is a challenge to love and trust when there is a significant risk that we will get hurt. In many cases, the hurt that comes from relationships is not a direct result of malice or ill intent. However, it is something we must still guard against. Trust is a prerequisite for love in the context of a relationship but we must always be cognizant of a person's ulterior motives. We all make mistakes and this is no reason to condemn a potential mate. However, there is a difference between simple mistakes and a pattern of misconduct. If something seems off, it may be appropriate to look more critically at your love interest's behavior to potentially identify red flags.

In the same vein, it is important to learn from past mistakes without punishing others for them. We discussed forgiveness in chapter 4, so here we want to simply reinforce its importance. Perhaps you were cheated on in a past relationship. Despite how hurtful it is and how much it may have shattered your faith in men, it would not be reasonable to assume that all men are cheating dogs. Adopting this mindset instantly distances you from anyone attempting to connect with you and can be terribly frustrating as you are punishing them for others' poor choices.

This falls in line with forgiveness which is another quality we must all adopt. As we mentioned before, we have all made mistakes. We are all sinners in the eyes of the Lord and we deserve death for our transgressions. The good news is that God saw fit to send his son to atone for our sins; a gift of forgiveness we are all undeserving of. While we, of course, are not God, we as Christians strive to be God-like. We exemplify our Christian values through our behavior and forgiveness is no different.

We mentioned earlier that the journey of life is one we should pack light for. Carrying past hurts and holding grudges can weigh us down to the point where it crushes us; making it impossible to move forward.

Letting go of the hurt and anger we harbor is especially challenging when the person who hurt us has not offered an apology. However, forgiveness is ultimately about our wholeness and wellbeing. Forgiving someone does not require that we see that individual. It can be a very personal action we do in our heart. Likewise, we may need to forgive ourselves for past mistakes. Living life with regret and beating ourselves up over our poor past decisions keeps us focused on the past. But focusing on the past can rob our future.

Great Communication Leads to a Great Relationship

IF TRUST IS THE FOUNDATION of a relationship, communication is undoubtedly its pillars. We are a collaborative species and the ability to communicate at high levels is what separates us from other animals. The power of spoken word cannot be understated as God Himself spoke the universe into being. Words give form to our ideas and feelings, making the abstract concrete. Appropriate communication is vital in any setting, but in the context of a relationship, it more often than not determines its success. A 2013 article from the Huffington Post cited poor communication as the number one cause for divorce according to a survey of one hundred mental health professionals. Seventy percent of the professionals surveyed said their male clients cited, nagging and complaining as the primary communication issue. Men hate nagging because it makes them feel as if the work they do is not good enough. They often work hard to ensure their wife is provided for and they perceive nagging as an invalidation of that hard work. Does this mean you should stop bringing issues up to your boyfriend, fiancé or husband? Absolutely not! Timing and technique are powerful when it comes to addressing issues. Even more powerful is prevention through proactive communication. We will start here.

Many of us have an expectation that our significant other will automatically know what our expectations and desires are. The reasoning is that someone in a relationship with us should know us well enough to be able to understand and meet our needs. Another rationale is that our thought processes make sense to us so they should be logical to everyone. These two rationales are flawed because they do not account for the fact that we all perceive and interpret the world differently (we discussed this in chapter 4). What makes sense to you may not make sense to your significant other. The problem is that many of us use these rationales as an excuse to avoid communicating our wants and needs. This creates a disconnect between expectations and reality leading to dissatisfaction, which leads to complaining, nagging, and arguments. While not all arguments can be avoided, clearly communicating expectations early on can help prevent unnecessary stress and heartache. Below are a few points on communication that you can incorporate into your current or future relationship to help make life easier.

Do Not Force Your Significant Other to Read Your Mind

WE HAVE ALREADY MENTIONED this but we all come from different backgrounds and experiences. We perceive the world differently and thus do not all think alike. Your significant other will not automatically know how you feel about something or what your desires are pertaining to it. Failing to communicate your desires leads to frustration on both sides. For you, it is upsetting that your significant other is not meeting your expectations. For your significant other, it's discouraging because, despite their best efforts, you are still unhappy.

Have a Serious Conversation About Roles and Responsibilities.

THIS MAY COME AS A surprise, but research shows that, there has been an increase in the percentage of stay at home dads in the U.S. over the past thirty years. This is significant in the context of communication because it denotes the fluidity of roles in dating, marriage, and child rearing. The "traditional" role of the man as the breadwinner and the woman as the one who takes care of the home is no longer a given. Often, tasks associated with each role are shared among a couple; especially when they both work. Bills, housekeeping, yardwork, child rearing and the tasks associated with them can be easily managed if you discuss them with your significant other and come up with a strategy on how you can tackle them together. Remember, life is a collaboration. Working with your significant other to attack tasks together instead of trying to stick to rigid roles will draw you closer together because it will feel like you are both helping one another instead of being forced to complete tasks.

If this feels challenging when you are in a committed relationship, it likely seems next to impossible when you are dating. It probably sounds silly to define roles on a date and we are not suggesting you pull your date aside and start strategizing how you're going to tackle dinner. In the same vein, you should avoid adhering to specific gender roles on dates. There are toxic perceptions in the dating world that can make dating feel very transactional. For example, the man should take the woman out and pay for the date. In return, the woman should offer her time, attention, and in some cases, body as payment. This can skew expectations and make for a very hostile experience, even if the hostility is all internal. Each person is focused on what they can get from the other, while giving up as little as possible in exchange. This attitude will bomb a date and sink a relationship before it can ever gain any momentum. Best-case scenario, the guy may simply seem agreeable during the date and never call you again because he picked up on the lack of effort or commitment on your part.

An alternative to this is approaching the date from a collaborative standpoint. Take an active role in the planning of the date; giving input on your preferences and places that may be suitable based on your date's input. Be prepared to contribute financially to at least a portion of the date. We like two-part dates or ones where two transactions occur because it allows both people to contribute without splitting the costs evenly (e.g. movies where one person covers the movie and the other covers the snacks). Show gratitude where you can by thanking them for spending time with you and money on you. Drive the conversation using the techniques we discussed in chapter 4 to learn more about the person and connect with them. If you get physical, ensure it is something that you both want and it is not something you feel pressured to do. Though casual sex is common in our society, it is important to remember that it is much more meaningful when reserved for your spouse. Ultimately, it loses its value if performed outside of marriage. If your end goal in dating is to find a life partner, let sex be something you reserve for them; and only when rings are exchanged.

> *"Let marriage be held in honor among all, and let the marriage bed be undefiled, for God will judge the sexually immoral and adulterous."*

Hebrews 13:4

We want to make clear that gender roles do matter in dating and relationships but not in the same way we have made them out to in the past. There tends to be confusion about this as we take passages like Ephesians 5:21-24 quite literally.

> *"Submit to one another out of reverence for Christ. Wives, submit to your husbands as to the Lord. For the husband is the*

head of the wife as Christ is the head of the church, his body, of
which he is the Savior. Now as the church submits to Christ, so
also wives should submit to their husbands in everything."

We have a tendency to forget the first piece that tells us to "submit to one another". Instead, many assume that women are somehow subordinate and inferior to men. But submission does not equal subordination or inferiority. Men are placed at the head of the household because there is an expectation that men lead. However, leadership is not about rule, but service and sacrifice. Christ leads and guides the church but the cost of this was his service in life and loving sacrifice on the cross. In exchange for this, we as the church give him our love and devotion and submit to his leadership. Likewise, a man must be prepared to give of himself in sacrifice to his relationship and family. This sacrificial love is what makes him worthy of the love and devotion of a woman. Likewise, a woman should be prepared to reciprocate this love through submission to service by serving him in turn and trusting him to lead the household. This is in itself a sacrifice because the woman is placing her trust in someone other than herself or God. Keeping all this in mind, we want to emphasize that these roles described in the Bible do not directly translate to societal roles. A submissive wife can still be the breadwinner while the stay at home dad can still be the leader of the household. We tend to tie leadership and dominance to finances but when we do this, we fail to see the whole picture.

Because relationships are a collaboration, it is vital that couples communicate heavily to ensure individual and relationship needs are being met. Remember, men and women were made to complement one another so we must work together to have a healthy relationship. Considering how fluid roles are, it is no surprise that contributions will not always be equal. Expecting that a relationship will always be 50/50 primes us for disappointment. Our lives are simply too complicated for there to be perfectly equal contribution all the time. And neither party should be keeping a tally of who paid for what and who went the furthest out of their way; as that drives the relationship away from harmony and selflessness and into an egocentric mass of tit for tat.

At times, we will have to give more to supplement our partner and vice versa. This is absolutely reasonable in a mutually supportive relationship as both parties are giving their all for the good of each other. In marriage, God intended us to be one flesh, one spirit, which means our contributions to the relationship ultimately benefit our singular being. In this, if both individuals are giving all they can, neither will ever think the other is holding back. This is another point where communication matters because your significant other may not see that you are struggling. While it may feel great for your significant other to always know when you're having difficulty and respond accordingly, it is unrealistic; more akin to that romance media we discussed in chapter 4.

This may all seem like a lot, but we are just scratching the surface of what it takes to have a healthy fulfilling relationship. The fruit we bear communicates what the gospel looks like lived out in the lives of Christians in marriage. But it even more significantly creates a relationship environment that glorifies God and grows us beautifully.

Summary

JUST BECAUSE YOU CAN'T undo *what* has affected you doesn't mean you can't undo *how* it has affected you. Further, it doesn't mean we can't end the cycle of brokenness that has plagued us our entire lives. A large part of living as a more whole person is about our interactions with other people. In this chapter, we discussed the second fold of our existence: production. What we produce and release into the world will significantly impact people's perception of us and has major implications for our relationships. To ensure the best possible outcome, we must have an understanding of five qualitative views:

- View Life as a Collaboration and Not a Competition
  - Relationships are not a zero-sum game
  - A spirit of collaboration will draw people to you
- Try to view issues from the perspective of the other person
  - Apply empathy to better understand others
  - Actively listen
- Exemplify the Qualities You Want to Attract
  - Don't be afraid to be yourself
  - Project positivity to attract other positive people
- Understand that No One is Perfect
  - Avoid holding potential mates to an impossible checklist
  - Use Degrees of Attraction to determine those traits most important to you
  - Trust, But Verify
- Realize that Great Communication Leads to Great Relationships
  - Don't' Make People Read Your Mind
  - Have a Serious Conversation About Roles in Your Relationship
  - Biblical gender roles and societal gender roles are not necessarily the same

Which of the five qualitative views just mentioned do you feel that you've struggled most with?

What next step(s) can you take to start (or continue) resolving your struggle with this view?

———————————

Chapter 6: Our Journey Continues

———

B y this point, we can all imagine the various ways in which we've not only experienced brokenness, but also the many ways in which we've acted out as a result of our desire for proof of love. Whether it takes the form of any of those "seven deadly sins" (pride, envy, gluttony, greed, lust, wrath, or sloth), these are all reactions to the unfulfilled need for love. And when these translate into the way we show and accept love, a multitude of negative styles of love might emerge. We might be the jealous lover or the impatient and selfish lover.

We might ignore our own needs and place our entire focus on pleasing others in an effort not to become distant or abandoned lovers. Or perhaps we might get fed up with feeling abandoned and alone and tell ourselves that we don't want or need anyone's love. But, in the end, all we're really doing is denying the truth. Just as God is love, we—His most precious creation; made in His image—also need love to thrive and flourish mentally, emotionally, spiritually, and even physically. Science attests to the many ways our most love filled moments benefit us psychologically and physically. The main way we experience this love as a gift from others is through their actions. Their actions prove to us that we are loved and treasured in their hearts. The unfortunate truth is that our need for this proof of love can actualize itself in any number of ways. And because we all have our own unique perspectives, inherent behaviors, and learned behaviors, our responses to our own desires (or to someone else's desires) can create conflicts that only worsen the signs and symptoms of brokenness.

So, what should our next step be? As with the resolution steps for any condition or scenario, it is first important to identify the issue for what it is. And in order to do this, you must spend the time required to identify the root cause. If life is like a game (as the proverb states) this is the part where you must put in the effort until you make a breakthrough, and no one else can do this part for you. It must be you.

Thankfully, there is more than one way to accomplish this. Prayer and fasting offer a very beneficial aid in uncovering some of the emotions and grudges held in the heart and the body. Psalm 139:23-25 reads,

> *"Search me, God, and know my heart;*
>
> *test me and know my anxious thoughts.*
>
> *See if there is any offensive way in me,*
>
> *and lead me in the way everlasting."*

The same can be said for meditating in a quiet place where you can ask God those vital questions. Examples would be:

- "Can you please show me who I haven't been treating as fairly (or lovingly) as I myself?"
- "Please Lord, I ask that you show me where I hold resentment toward others and help me to understand why."
- "If I have thought or acted negatively toward any family, friends, or acquaintances this week, can you please help me to uncover that which I was not able to notice before?"

Once you ask this question (or these questions), many of us would think to continue asking or to dust our hands, say "Nope. No one came to mind. Guess I'm good," and proceed to say a prayer of thanks before continuing on with our regularly scheduled program. But this is not a time to rush answers or keep speaking until the Lord quiets you with an angelic epiphany. God doesn't tend to have a shouting contest with us. It is quite the opposite. When we stop talking and start listening for long enough, the answers can finally come.

How long is long enough? As long as it takes. Patience and stillness are key here. Remember you are sitting and communing with the Lord. So, what's the rush. Be in His presence and be as patient as you need to be for as many days as you need to come back and ask for insight. Whether you receive revelations within the first sixty seconds or after ten days, they will come.

Remember that it took some time for your reactions to that lacking proof of love to develop. Equally, there was a process of you learning to hide that brokenness from others and yourself. So, it should reason that you might not uncover it all immediately. But the important ray of light here is that you can uncover and resolve it. You can also have very frank moments with those you love and trust. Ask them about some of the behaviors you display that are not pleasant. Dig deep about areas in your life that they think you can work as it deals with relating to them and others. You may be surprised to hear similar issues arise, or issues that share the same root cause. Make sure not to take the moments as an attack but a wonderful opportunity for change.

The four pillars of whole love are necessary to everyone, but in varied amounts. These pillars are presence, offerings, loving touch, and verbal unification. And although everyone benefits from each of these pillars, we all have a dominant one that we need to experience more abundantly than the other three pillars. Again, this is a form of proof that we not only hold value as individuals, but that we are worthy of love. The unfortunate truth is that although we are all worthy of love and should be aware of our own self-worth, it is very easy to question this truth and look outside of ourselves for proof that this isn't some delusional notion we're all quietly carrying. This proof we're seeking is what we refer to as proof of love.

With adequate proof of love, we develop from childhood into adulthood and flourish as individuals and as collective communities. But without it, we lash out at others—and even at ourselves—in a desperate attempt to either create a value we never knew was there or to convince ourselves and others that we don't care whether or not we are considered valuable.

But the truth of the matter is that we do care. But that isn't something to be ashamed of. It is something to be revered and celebrated because it is one more beautiful part of God's design. And it works somewhat like a compass that helps us to see if we're thriving on the love we're experiencing or if some part of that love is in need of a subtle yet powerful course correction.

As the saying goes, "it's the little things." We often look to the little things—things that shouldn't require some grand effort—to prove to us and remind us that we have significant value and that we are worthy children of God. And we have been ever since God himself decreed it so and sent His only son as a sacrifice to prove it.

And therein lies our God-given power. The power to throw off the shackles that the enemy placed over our hearts when we were distracted. The shackles that prevent us from easily seeing a way out. But, let us say once more that there is a way out. There is a way that God provided for us to be filled with love and to give love to others; knowing that it is so overflowing and abundant that we could never hope to run out. This love is one of the many blessings God has bestowed on us; His children. And—like His forgiveness—this blessing can never reach its end. And that is because God's love is eternal.

As we progress in our healing, we will begin to example the truth of the Scriptures in our actions and interactions with others. As Ephesians 4:2-3 states:

"Be completely humble and gentle; be patient, bearing with one another in love. Make every effort to keep the unity of the Spirit through the bond of peace."

It goes without saying that we will experience hardships that put a serious strain on our sense of humility. Just as we can uncover truths about our unmet needs when we stop trying to reason away our less than ideal behavior, our interactions with others can also reveal how much progress we've made with pouring into ourselves with the love of God exemplified in the pillars of whole love. And, perhaps even more importantly, we can begin to ask ourselves how we can example the love and harmony of God amongst our brothers and sisters in the way that God intended. Not the way that makes us feel like we got the last word in or achieved the last laugh. We can learn to continually attune our actions to that of a faithful servant that we know in our hearts would make God proud. If your actions with others aren't accomplishing that, then chances are that you (just like all of us) still have some work to do. Thankfully, God has and continues to make a way. But you must put in the effort and energy to build that Godly love within yourself and use it for your benefit and for the benefit of others. Look to Hebrews 10:24, and see how it means to direct our actions by saying:

> *"And let us consider how we may spur one another on towards love and good deeds."*

We know the journey is a long and treacherous one. And we know that sometimes it gets scary to ask those questions, hear those answers from God, and know that you must hold yourself accountable for doing the work necessary to achieve righteousness in your actions and harmony with your brothers and sisters in Christ. But fear cannot be our motivator in this life. Fear is not God's way; love is. As it says in 1 John 4:18,

"There is no fear in love. But perfect love drives out fear, because fear has to do with punishment. The one who fears is not made perfect in love."

Approaching Wholeness from an Outside Point of View

JUST AS WE DISCUSSED in chapter 1, it is important to sit quietly and take the time to ask God for guidance and then listen for His answer. Think back to situations in which you may have slighted someone and ask yourself, "If I were in that person's shoes, what response would have kept me from feeling slighted or insulted?" Once you have your answer, hold yourself accountable with treating that person (and all people for that matter) in the same way you would like to be treated. If you do not like to be insulted, make a point not to insult others. If you would not like to be openly scorned or scoffed at, challenge yourself not to exhibit that behavior with another person. If relationships were regularly approached in this way, we would argue that many of those failed romances—even familial or friendly bonds that weakened and eventually fell apart—would've held strong and maintained a fighting chance even in the face of adversity.

By recognizing who God is, who God says you are, and using prayer as a means of finding our spiritual freedom, we can not only find the answers we need, but we can also move with a sense of certainty; knowing that we are being directed by the love of God. And through that love, healing, reconciliation, and an abundant life are more than possible. They are our birthright!

Love is meant for all of us. It nurtures our minds as children and feeds our hearts well into adulthood. God's love is unwavering and without flaws of any kind. It is perfect. And in the perfection of God's love for us, we are also blessed with the opportunity to share our love with others. We are able to commune with our family and friends. We are able to make new friends and grow our family. And just as we desire, God has created many windows of opportunity for us to find a special someone with whom we can create a family of our own, rather than being forced to accept any number of toxic relationships.

In your waiting for that special someone, we would like to share some words of encouragement and notions to bear in mind. We've gleaned these little nuggets of wisdom from others over the years and they've greatly helped us in our journey so far. We truly hope they serve as a benefit to you in some way as well.

Tip #1: If you have a FULLER UNDERSTANDING of what love is, you will understand if what you are actually giving and receiving is love or simply fleeting admiration

1 Corinthians 13: 4-8 says,

> *"Love is patient, love is kind. It does not envy, it does not boast, it is not proud. It does not dishonor others, it is not self-seeking, it is not easily angered, it keeps no record of wrongs. Love does not delight in evil but rejoices with the truth. It always protects, always trusts, always hopes, always perseveres. Love never fails."*

Many of us say might believe that we are showing others love all the time. But we should challenge ourselves to continually improve our personal understanding of what love is and how we can best show it to ourselves and to others. When we become short, jealous, or angered by those we say we love, we are often showing little more than basic tolerance. We probably all have a few family members or friends that get into arguments with each other all the time because they can't help but keep a record of all the times they were wronged by one another. And when your relationship is rooted in a history of keeping a tally of all that you've done for someone else or of all the times they've mistreated you, that relationship will be a far cry from what the word of God describes as love.

Tip #2 Love Conquers All

1 Peter 4:8 says,

> *"Above all, love each other deeply, because love covers over a multitude of sins."*

This is a great example of how powerful love is. When love is introduced into the picture, healing, forgiveness, and spiritual growth is more than possible. Remember that God is love, and if God directs your actions there can only be good things to come as a result.

Tip #3 Treat others the way YOU want to be treated

Matthew 7:12 says,

> *"So, in everything, do unto others what you would have them do to you..."*

This might seem about as clichéd as the previous tip, but it's no less true. The more we stop to ask ourselves if that next thing we're about to say or action we're too ready to take would rub us the wrong way before continuing on, the less likely we are to create wedges in our existing relationships or ruin our chances at creating new relationships before they can begin. It's easy to say that someone else is just being petty, needy, soft, or jealous in response to something we say or do. But the fact of the matter is that if the tables were turned and that same someone else acted that way toward us, we would be hurt, livid, dismissive, or worse. And when your desire is to create a strong and lasting relationship with someone else, it is important to be yourself. But it's just as important to be the kind of person you would want to be around.

Bonus Tip - As you think and act, so shall you have and so shall you be

This may sound like another version of the fake it until you make it axiom, but it's actually very different. Instead of pretending to be something that you know you aren't, we would advise that you work to exemplify a life that identifies you by the traits you most highly respect in other women. If you respect patient people, challenge yourself to be more patient. If you highly admire women who command the same respect that they give, then work toward becoming that type of woman.

Some of you might think this is easier said than done or that this is so easy that you will accomplish this in a single day. But let us refer to another saying. Rome wasn't built in one day. This saying has a two-fold meaning.

First fold: This means that the grander the task or potential outcome, the greater the time and concerted effort will generally be required. So, don't expect any miracles here (no pun intended) only to get discouraged if the end result isn't achieved immediately.

Second fold: Whether it took months or years, Rome was eventually built. Let this notion encourage you that despite the task at hand, if you refuse to give up and keep your trust in the Lord, it will eventually come to pass.

That being said, we would encourage all women to carry themselves in a manner befitting both a lady and a woman of God. When a woman acts like a lady, her man will not only be proud to have her at his side, but he will also treat her like the lady that he knows her to be as a result of her actions. When we think of the characteristics of a lady, we often think of someone who nurtures and supports others. Someone who is generally patient and caring. Someone who understands how to show respect and is therefore also respected. Someone who is not promiscuous or confrontational to the point of combative. She is knowledgeable, appreciative, considerate, and an absolute pleasure to be around. It is this type of lady that we both look up to and lean on, because this type of woman is a pillar of the household and the community in her own right.

We'll leave you with one additional scripture to ponder and meditate on. Our hope is that if you're reading this then that means that you are also committing yourself to putting in the work to be the kind of woman mentioned in Proverbs 31:10-11:

> *"A wife of noble character who can find? She is worth far more than rubies. Her husband has full confidence in her and lacks nothing of value."*

It's About Purpose

IT ALWAYS HAS, IS, and will be about purpose. We used most of this book to talk about brokenness and healing but why? So you're able to develop the right qualities to snag the right man? Wrong. The aim of this book is to help you realize that God wants to use you for His Glory. He wants your life to be a testament of His goodness, but how? God's ultimate purpose is to reconcile men unto Him. He wants a beautiful and harmonious relationship with mankind. Christ has made this reconciliation possible through yielding himself as an atonement for our sins. This sacrifice gives us the ability to not only be right with God but represent God on Earth. Take a look at that word again, RE PRE-SENT. God wants to show Himself to the world through us, this is our purpose. When we allow our brokenness to define us, we are actually fracturing and distorting the image of God that we were designed to display. However, when we walk in His newness and healing we reflect His whole image; one that is true, faithful, and unbroken. Any relationship we find ourselves in should be an opportunity to fulfill God's purpose in our lives and interestingly enough, relationships in and of themselves scream the heart of God. So yes, walking in purpose will make you a better wife, sister, and friend but more importantly, it allows the world to see whose daughter you are.

Final Thoughts

WE'VE COVERED QUITE a bit here; including the romantic struggles of our Dana, Brittany, Meghan, and Rhonda. As you can see, missing one or more pillars of whole love for too long can easily influence undesirable behavior. By now, our hope is that at least one of their stories struck a chord with you and what you may have experienced (or may be currently experiencing). The thought processes and reactions to what each of these women felt they were missing were not rooted in the same wholeness that God's love harbors. And so, as a result of less than healthy responses to their desires for proof of love, each of these women experienced increasing hardship in fulfilling their need to feel both whole and loved.

But there is always a way out of despair. Through the death and resurrection of His Son — God has seen to it that we can accomplish great things and become whole through His love and grace alone. But that also means we need to stop and check ourselves to ensure that the path we're treading is in line with His will. If our steps are ordered in His word, we can come out of any adversity. And so, we will challenge you with one final task. Together we will take a bird's-eye look at their situations and choose healthy and whole-minded next steps for them.

Dana

Dana came from a home that lacked loving touch and verbal unification (her dominant pillars of whole love), and she tended to try and control the men in her relationships. She was clingy and defensive, and the way she acted out drove both potential mates and friends away. The older Dana got, the harder it became for her to connect with people; as no one seemed to appreciate her blunt nature or the effort she put into remaining loyal and committed to her relationships. She felt that she shouldn't have to change who she was and that a good man would see her for the diamond in the rough that she was. But her thirtieth birthday was just around the corner, and it looked like the next year of her life would be as lonely and disappointing as the previous one.

Approaching this from a standpoint of wholeness, what would you recommend as Dana's best next steps, and why?

A. Try and online dating service. Studies show that there are more and more successful relationships coming from online dating, because there are fewer barriers to finding so many people worldwide. And it's possible that God has ordained this as an easier way for Dana to meet the person that He's prepared for her.

B. Keep doing what she's been doing. There's nothing wrong with her approach, and she just needs a little more time.

C. Reflect on her actions and ask God to help her understand where she can improve. Then, make a list of traits describing how she sees herself, and ask a few friends she trusts to tell her if she comes across in that way when interacting with them and others.

Your Reasoning:

Brittany

We mentioned that Brittany highly values presence from those she cared about, and that she continually lowered her standards for potential mates in order to keep from being alone. Brittany constantly seemed to be putting all of her eggs in one basket with each new guy she met. But that kept ending in disappointment for one reason or another as her first thought was always, "Is this the one?" Over time, Brittany became less and less picky and was almost willing to settle for any guy with a friendly smile and a pulse; no matter how tepid the relationship was. But deep down, she knew that she wouldn't be any happier with just any guy than she would be with no one.

Approaching this from a standpoint of wholeness, what would you recommend as Brittany's best next steps, and why?

    A. Spend some time focusing on what makes her happy and doing an online search for people who have similar interests.

    B. Remind herself that God wouldn't haphazardly place her into any relationship and that she should remove her focus from what she doesn't have and focus more on appreciating all the things that she does have.

    C. Put out an ad in the paper and see who bites.

Your Reasoning:

Meghan

Meghan was the type of person who loved being the center of attention. She was lacking in offerings and presence from the people she cared about, and sought to achieve major accomplishments as a way to shore up what was missing in her life. She figured if she could achieve something great then she wouldn't even have to try to get acknowledgement from others. This translated over to her job; where she often went above and beyond for fear of letting anyone down. But the long hours that her recent promotion required had placed so much of a strain on her relationship that her boyfriend couldn't take it. He gave her an ultimatum of either make sacrifices with her job or losing her relationship with him.

Approaching this from a standpoint of wholeness, what would you recommend as Meghan's best next steps, and why?

A. Download a few dating apps and see what happens.
B. Write down the reasons she really wants to keep both her current boyfriend and her job. Then, go through what she believes she will need to give up for each. Once this is all written down, she can meditate on both options and ask herself, based on what she's seen so far, what kind of life she honestly believes she will live with the boyfriend or the job five or ten years from now. If she needs further insight, she can reach out to people she trusts or engage in prayer for guidance.
C. Ask her pastor for guidance on the matter and be willing to accept the answers provided.

Your Reasoning:

Rhonda

Rhonda really wanted loving touch throughout her childhood. But being one of five children living in a single-parent home, hugs and undivided attention were in very short supply. Rhonda was a high-achiever in school. And that translated over to her friendships; where she generally came to relish in the fact that she was the responsible one. But for all her responsibility, she couldn't fill the void that seemed to continually resurface in all of her romantic relationships. Her lack of patience with men tended to bring every relationship she had to an abrupt close; usually due to a lack of open communication or suffering some disappointment in the guy she was dating. And so, she quickly moved on to the next one, or just outright cheated with another guy. But no matter how many men she dated, it never seemed to work out for some reason.

Approaching this from a standpoint of wholeness, what would you recommend as Rhonda's best next steps, and why?

A. Rhonda should look into taking an anger management workshop

B. Look to join a group or seminar for people who like to lead and learn better ways to be a leader.

C. Rhonda will need to admit her faults and ask herself if she would endure a relationship where the guy she was with acted like she does in relationships. Then, she should ask herself what she feels is most lacking in her life and why. Based on her honest answer, Rhonda can seek counseling from her pastor, a qualified professional, or simply start focusing on all the positive lessons and good things that came from dating, and challenge herself to begin vocalizing her needs to those she trusts and focusing on approaching all future dating from a 'do unto others' mindset once she feels confident in her ability to do so. Until then, she should NOT be dating.

Your Reasoning:

*One note to keep in mind here is that it is possible that there is more than one right answer. But the reasoning portion is open-ended so that you have the opportunity to elaborate on your answer. There's a good chance that this will reveal more about the way that you think and approach problems for the sake of addressing similar matters in your life.

We truly hope that this portion of the chapter provided some great additional insight for you. If any part of this and the rest of the book can be applied to the enrichment and improvement of your life, then the purpose of this book has been fulfilled.

On the next page, you will find our answers and our reasoning behind the answers.

Dana: C

Our Reasoning:

It is not uncommon for us to fail to see our faults. Sometimes we don't want to see them. But if we aren't honest with ourselves we cannot hope to improve ourselves or our situation. Before stating that the problem lies with someone else, we should always be willing to ask ourselves what we might be doing to add to the problem and be willing to answer honestly. If we cannot find the answer, we may need to look to others we trust to provide those answers or at least to provide some additional insight from their perspective. Again, the focus here is what we can do for ourselves to improve ourselves. Not how we can prove that we're in the right. Because that will just give us more of what we've already got and don't want.

Brittany: B

Our Reasoning:

Brittany needs to understand her value in the eyes of God and use that understanding to fuel her own sense of self-worth. Anything that is highly valued will not be taken lightly or placed in situations that could potentially pull away from its value. Brittany should treat her heart and her time in much the same manner. That doesn't mean that she should hold herself above any man who approaches her. But it does mean that if she knows that she isn't happy with that person because they treat her with the love and respect that she should be giving herself, then she needs to move on and be patient with attracting the kind of man that will. If she carries herself in a way that shows her value and self-worth, then that will be more attractive than accepting any old relationship.

Meghan: B (or possibly C)

Our Reasoning:

Meghan needs to understand what most matters to her and place herself first (after God, of course) in this scenario. If she can foresee a future with her current job that adds to want she want s out of life more than what her boyfriend adds and he cannot accept that, then chances are that they aren't meant for one another. The same goes vice versa, But this needs to be understood before making any big decisions she might regret. And if she cannot figure this out for herself, perhaps her pastor or another person she trusts can help her to better understand this.

Rhonda: C

Our Reasoning:

'True healing can't begin until you take stock of what you've done to contribute to a problem. Without that awareness, you would be unable to resolve the issue. This is a lesson that Dana needs to learn and apply to her own situation. If she can understand where she is in her life and how SHE is potentially keeping herself in that place, she can start developing a way out.

This may not be as easy as it sounds (and trust us, it doesn't sound easy for most), but if she needs help with this, she should feel comfortable with turning to someone she trusts for wisdom and candid insight. With knowledge comes power. With the application of knowledge comes wisdom.

From Ezekiel and Kiyanna

WE CAN'T BELIEVE WE'RE here now, 11 years later with 5 children to show for it. It's safe to say we've had our fair share of ups and downs but our downs seemed to characterize the first few years of our marriage. If we had stumbled across this book before we said I do, we would've been able to easily spot out the glaring issues within us and sought help before proceeding.

I (Ezekiel) had no idea I was a fearful lover. My insecurities stemmed from childhood, where I lacked the pillars of loving touch and verbal unification. I wanted to be loved but was so afraid of rejection I would keep Kiyanna from seeing my weaknesses in order to keep up the facade of strength. I would respond with silent anger, stubborn intellectual arguments, and even escape to pornography so that I didn't have to deal with the 'me' I was trying to keep Kiyanna from finding — the broken me — the real me.

And While I (Kiyanna) thought he was Prince Charming, all of his insecurities begin to spill out violently at once like a bursting pipe. I couldn't believe that he didn't count me as close enough to be vulnerable with me from the beginning. But I had my own baggage that I didn't want him to help me carry. I was an insecure lover. Lacking the pillar of true presence, I wasn't given enough security in the love I wanted to receive as a child. My relationship before I met Ezekiel was disastrous, I gave way too much of my heart and time to a guy who proved undeserving of it. I thought God gave me Ezekiel, the perfect guy, to make up for the junk I just dealt with, but that wasn't the case. I often made Ezekiel feel guilty for not filling a void that wasn't his job to fill. Arguments and silent wars didn't make any of it better. We realized that maybe the problem wasn't that our relationship wasn't working but we forgot to work on ourselves before we came together. And that's the purpose of this book. We want you as the reader to take time to uncover your current brokenness, figure out how you got here and take steps to heal. We don't want you to make the same mistakes we did; dragging old problems into new relationships. So if you're single, stop, read this book and heal. If you're in a relationship stop, read this book and heal. The God that keeps you is at work, leading you towards His purpose. God wants you healed! And if you're truly grateful for God's hand on your life, you will be serious about making sure your vessel is fit to carry whatever He's preparing.

After much prayer, marriage counseling, individual counseling, wisdom from

Spiritual leaders and constant communication with each other, we have grown tremendously. We have learned from our past trauma and are celebrating this journey of wholeness that we are sharing with you today.

But we have to be completely honest. We have new mountains and new battles with demons that seemed to have only showed up once we said 'I do'. There is so much to share that we would have to write another book to do it justice, and that's exactly what we will do.

Be prepared for the next book in the series, "The Whole Marriage", where we share our challenges but also the keys towards a real but God honoring marriage. We can't wait to see what God continues in your life and the impact your new-found wholeness will have on

your loved ones.

Before you set this book down we want to share with you and excerpt from my (Ezekiel's) poem *Chemotherapy*. May you use it as a reminder of the darkness of the pit of brokenness you've been rescued from and the brilliant light that has consumed you today.

Emotional Chemotherapy

HOW LONG, WILL YOU protect your shambles from the spiritual physician

You can't treat cancer of the soul on your own

Cuz without the shedding of blood, there is no remission

Can you smell it?

The stale odor of Eden in this room?

God is asking where are you?

Not because he's unaware of location

Or because he needs more understanding when you explain your situation

He's teaching you to embrace the beauty of honest confrontation

God's questions are just mirrors provoking self-examination

Where are you?

You've hidden behind your ways long enough

It's time to surrender the fig leaves

Your father's sacrifice alone is sufficient to cover you completely...

So let go, my brother, he knows you better than you know yourself;

You've been addicted long enough,

Made excuses, sinned in vain, with syringes

Long enough

Let go, my sister, you've suffered at their hands, do not suffer at your own

No new job, home or man

Can gift you beauty for the ashes you've known

And what you've given your life to

Is not what he gave his life for

But you're not God enough to fix it

You can't redeem what you didn't die for

So yes it happened, yes it hurt you

But it is not you, cuz it's not worth you

And here; herein lies the ultimate test of your theology

When God calls you to forgive someone without expecting their apology

Let go

Let go and

Don't let garbage overtake you

Let go please let go

You can't let

grudges overcome you

Grip on to what the Gospel offers you

And it could guillotine the obstacles

Give opportunity for the

Glorious omnipotent

God to operate

If the gracious one got ownership

Tell the devil to get off of it

God's grabbing you out

the grave, offering life

Saying GET ON with it!

For there is good news, the radiation from the trauma we've suffered through did not kill us

because the body belongs to God

Our weakness gave Him

Reason to be strong for us along

We are more than survivors

Because the definition of survive simply means 'not dead'

Though that may be worth the

Flight of our hands in praises

It's a temporary visa, not a state we're supposed to stay in

But he was wounded for our transgressions, he was bruised for our iniquities, and the Punishment for our peace was upon him, so by his stripes we are healed

To thrive,

Past the cancer that

Riddled our souls

So in his purpose rise and go

Because your faith has made you whole

About the Author

With over a decade of marriage under their belts, the Azonwu's are quickly becoming a household name amongst urban Christians. Husband and father Ezekiel born to Nigerian immigrants in Huntsville, Alabama and Kiyanna born in Los Angeles California seem like a couple brought together by purpose. Ezekiel is more widely known for his hard hitting Christian spoken word poems that have had a viral effect online. He founded the largest spoken word tour in history the Poets in Autumn Tour in 2015 featuring the biggest names in Christian Poetry. Kiyanna launched ThisisGlory LLC in 2018, a forum for hair growth and care which serves women internationally. Together they are passionate about the Gospel and showing the world what true love looks like. They currently live in Atlanta GA with their 5 children.

Read more at www.thewholelifenow.com.